The DSDM Atern Student Workbook

a guide to the definitive Agile framework

Published by

Galatea Training Services Limited
St John's Vicarage
The Avenue
High Legh
Knutsford
Cheshire
WA16 6ND

Tel: +44 (0)1706 351389
Email: info@galatea.co.uk
Website: www.galatea.co.uk

© D.J. & I.J. Tudor 2010

ISBN: 0-9543071-3-5
        978-0-9543071-3-4

CONTENTS

Foreword

As Chairman of the DSDM Consortium I am thrilled to be able to introduce this Student Workbook for DSDM Atern. It complements well the Atern Manual and the various pocketbooks available and will prove a great help to those wishing to understand the DSDM Atern framework.

I would like to thank the authors for their dedication and hard work in producing the Workbook which, I am sure, will prove invaluable to all who use it.

Steve Messenger
Chairman
DSDM Consortium

Preface

With the recent and rapid rise in interest in Agile approaches, it would not be unreasonable to assume that they are a new phenomenon. However, the origins of Agile approaches to projects can be found as far back as the early 1990s, in many disciplines ranging from software development right through to manufacturing.

The need for a more agile approach to solution development was driven by commercial pressures: the need to deliver outcomes from projects on-time and within budget, whilst focusing on business value. This emphasised the need for end-user involvement in projects in order to focus on the outcome required.

Early projects were beset with problems. Rapid Application Development tended to focus on 'quick wins' and was accused of delivering products in those early days that were christened 'quick and dirty' – these were both unmaintainable and of poor quality.

In response to the criticisms levelled at the approach, a group of very experienced professionals, from both large multinational companies through to SMEs, gathered together to share their experience in an unprecedented collaboration to further the drive for a repeatable, rapid approach (the term Agile had not yet been adopted). This collaboration gave birth to The DSDM Consortium. The Consortium was formed in 1994 and grew rapidly, soon rising to over a thousand member companies. It was named after the approach (Dynamic Systems Development Method) that it was destined to define.

Other approaches, such as Adaptive Software Development (ASD), Scrum, Extreme Programming (XP) and Crystal, collectively also known as Agile, have common agile elements but none has embodied the richness of content and the completeness of purpose that has been built into DSDM.

Whilst initially focusing on software projects, it has also been recognised that DSDM can be used on any type of project, where the purpose is to deliver business benefits quickly, reliably, predictably, to an appropriate level of quality and within a specific budget and timeframe. This universal applicability was recognised in the development and launch, during 2007, of the latest version of the approach, DSDM Atern, which forms the subject of this book.

Put simply, DSDM Atern works! We hope that this book will help to take you on a journey to change the way that your projects deliver, as it has for ours, and for many others...

1. Approach and Principles

1. What is DSDM Atern?

Dynamic Systems Development Method (DSDM) Atern is an Agile project delivery framework for business solutions. The fundamental purpose of DSDM Atern is to provide a framework for the development and deployment of business-supporting solutions which are delivered with high speed, high quality and within tight timescales. Typically, operational solutions are delivered into the working environment within three to six months and may be much sooner than this: deliveries are planned to be business-value driven, frequent and incremental. The aim is always to build and release the product in complete 'chunks', and to deliver something of value to the business as early as practicable.

DSDM Atern uses the following key techniques:

- MoSCoW prioritisation;
- Facilitated workshops;
- Iterative development;
- Modelling and prototyping;
- Timeboxing.

It also depends on:

- Business involvement throughout the project;
- Empowered, multi-skilled teams.

Earlier versions of DSDM were often associated with IT systems. However, it was always recognised that the approach is as applicable to any business change project whether or not there is an IT element. DSDM Atern is applicable to ALL types of project.

2. The Philosophy of DSDM Atern

The philosophy of DSDM Atern is that any project must be:

- Aligned to clearly-defined strategic goals;
- Focused on *early* delivery of *real* benefits to the business.

This is best achieved when key stakeholders understand the business objectives, are empowered to an appropriate level and collaborate with solution developers and each other in order to deliver the right solution, in the agreed timescales, according to priorities set by the business.

In order to gain the benefits of on time and on budget deliveries, stakeholders must be prepared to deliver a 'fit for purpose' solution, in increments, and accept that change is inevitable, as understanding of the requirements and the solution develop.

2.1 Flexing requirements

In direct contrast with some traditional approaches to solution development, DSDM Atern allows and expects requirements to evolve and change. In the DSDM Atern approach, time is fixed for the life of a project, and resources are fixed as far as possible. Therefore, in order to deliver what is required, both on time and in budget, the flexibility has to come from the ability to prioritise requirements as they are elicited during the early project phases and as they are refined during the project lifecycle.

What is DSDM Atern?

An Agile Project Delivery Framework that delivers the right solution at the right time

- Any kind of project
- Focused on business benefit
- On time and in budget
- Quality and rigour
- Incremental
- Collaborative

© TCC   DSATP/1/ 4

3. Deliver Something Working, Sooner Rather Than Later

It is often the case, in a project, that proportionately more time is taken to develop areas of the solution which will be used infrequently than to develop the essential functionality. A fundamental assumption of the DSDM Atern approach is that the whole solution does not necessarily need to be provided in the first release of the delivered product. As a rule of thumb, 80% of the solution can probably be produced in 20% of the time that it would take to produce the whole solution (Pareto Principle). If this 80% can be deployed, business value can be gained from it whilst the remaining features are being developed.

Traditionally, stakeholders are often asked to supply both current and future requirements. This rarely has the effect of 'future-proofing' the solution, since business requirements emerge as understanding increases and the business environment changes over time. DSDM Atern embraces the fact that we learn as we go and allows for detail to emerge later rather than sooner.

Experience has shown that the business requirements will probably change as understanding increases, so exhaustive early work can be wasted time. Since DSDM Atern assumes that previous steps can be revisited as part of its iterative approach, further work can be conducted later.

Although DSDM Atern embraces the fact that change will occur as a project progresses, it is also a convergent approach, clarifying the direction, benefits required, and solution architecture upfront. This makes it well-suited to large organisations with complex architectures, into which new developments must fit. It is very suitable for small, simple change projects, but it is also well-suited to large, complex projects.

DSDM Atern works for new solutions, development of enhancements, and deployment of 'off the shelf' solutions. It suits inhouse developments and working with external suppliers of solutions.

4. Prioritisation and MoSCoW

To make a promise to deliver on time and within cost, whilst keeping a focus on business need could mean that the quality of the deliverable would be compromised, unless we have some other flexibility. That flexibility can only come from the features we deliver, and may mean that some features that were originally envisaged have to be left out. The positive aspect to this is that if new, essential requirements emerge during the project, they can actually be considered for inclusion without threatening delivery deadline or cost.

In a DSDM Atern project, quite intentionally, requirements are not fully analysed at the outset of the project; therefore if a requirement does have *to be de-scoped, little work has been wasted on it.* This de-scoping is always by agreement of the appropriate stakeholders in the project and has a business-value focus. Each of the requirements identified in the Prioritised Requirements List (PRL) is regularly assessed for business criticality by the multi-skilled team made up of business and technical skills, and features can be prioritised for delivery according to business need and value. Some of the non-functional requirements, such as security, may also be classified as high priority.

'MoSCoW' prioritisation is a technique for helping to gain a common understanding of priorities. The letters stand for:

- **M**ust have;
- **S**hould have;
- **C**ould have;
- **W**on't have this time.

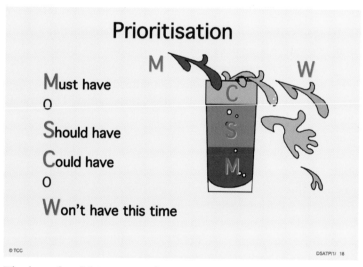

The benefit of this approach over classifications such as 'desirable', 'highly desirable', and 'showstopper', is in the definition of what will happen to a requirement in each classification, in terms of the delivered solution within a particular timeframe: for example, does 'highly desirable' mean that the solution is still useful without it? The following are the much clearer definitions based on MoSCoW:

Must haves are requirements that are fundamental to the system; without them the system will be unworkable or useless. The 'Must haves' define the minimum usable subset which the DSDM Atern project guarantees to satisfy.

Should haves are important requirements, but for which there is a workaround in the short term. These would normally be classed as mandatory in less time-constrained development, but the system will be useful and usable without them.

Could haves are requirements that would add some business benefit, but can be left out of the increment under development without serious consequences.

Won't have this time are still valuable requirements, but can wait until later development takes place.

The MoSCoW rules provide the basis on which decisions can be made about what will be developed during a Timebox, within an increment of the project, and over the project as a whole.

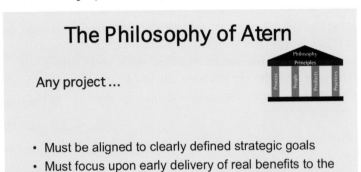

5. Where Did DSDM Atern Come From?

In the early 1990s, changes to the way in which business was conducted swept the world at an ever-increasing pace and the automation of business processes was widespread. Organisations were feeling increasing pressure to respond rapidly to market change and this meant being able to build or modify computer-supported systems within very short timeframes. Traditional approaches were focused on building maintainable, flexible systems, but gave unacceptably long lead times for any development. The result was a wave of 'quick and dirty' systems being put together which were costly to maintain and not sufficiently robust. There was a strong motivation from many organisations to improve the situation. The vendor-independent, not-for-profit DSDM Consortium was formed in Ashford, Kent, UK in January 1994, with the objective of developing and continuously evolving a public domain method for RAD (Rapid Application Development). Du Pont Fibres had already defined an approach called RIPP (Rapid I Production Prototyping) and James Martin had advocated the use of Timeboxes in his RAD approach.

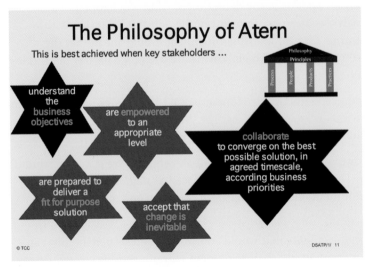

The DSDM approach was released early in 1995 (DSDM Version 1) based on best practices gained from a membership of suppliers and end-users of business systems, typically working in blue-chip companies. The approach gathered momentum and rapidly evolved to DSDM Version 2, published in late 1995. Version 3 was launched in September 1997 as the method continued to be refined. Version 4 was launched in October 2001.

DSDM always took a top-down view of projects, with techniques for governance and control, as well as for collaboration with the business sponsors and end-users. Meanwhile, a similar movement (eXtreme programming) was emerging in the United States. This came much more from the grass roots of software development, but focused on customer involvement, and on delivering something useful early. In 2001, a group of individuals from various approaches, including DSDM and Extreme Programming, met in Snowbird, Utah and defined the now well-known 'Agile Manifesto'. The term 'Agile' has been used ever since, to classify approaches with a high degree of customer involvement, a focus on business benefit and on delivering something functional and useful in a short timeframe.

In the early days, DSDM was a method for members only. In 2006, the DSDM method was declared 'open': free to view and free to use. The full method can be seen at www.dsdm.org.

DSDM Atern was launched in April 2007 and continues to evolve, as an Agile approach to all types of project.

6. The Benefits of DSDM Atern

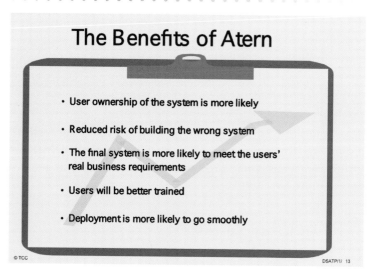

DSDM Atern uses an iterative approach to solution development and deployment. Users are actively involved throughout the whole development and deployment process and this brings with it many benefits:

- *The users are more likely to claim ownership for the solution.* They have been actively involved in defining the solution and feel it is theirs;

- *The risk of building the wrong solution is greatly reduced.* The involvement of real end users in DSDM Atern roles throughout the project, plus the visibility of elements of the evolving solution are a constant check on the solution that is being evolved;

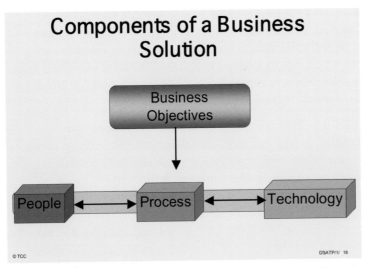

- *The final solution is more likely to meet the users' real business requirements.* The final solution emerges in increments and can be steered towards the real business need by adding to these elements, which are being used and experienced early in a real situation;

- *The users will be better trained, as their representatives have been involved throughout.* The user representatives within the solution development teams can help in the identification of those who will need training. They will also know the solution well and will be able to act as coaches in the business environment;

- *The deployment of the solution is more likely to go smoothly,* because of the teamwork involved. The user representatives in the team have a good relationship with the solution developers and know who to ask if things do not work as they should. Additionally, their knowledge of how the solution is meant to work is invaluable in the early days of its use.

7. The Eight Principles of DSDM Atern

DSDM Atern defines eight principles which are fundamental to the successful application of the approach. Compromising any principle undermines DSDM Atern's basic philosophy and constitutes a risk to the on time and on-budget delivery of the right solution.

The collective value of DSDM Atern's principles enables organisations to deliver best value business solutions collaboratively and consistently.

DSDM Atern's Eight Principles are:

1. Focus on the business need.

2. Deliver on time.

3. Collaborate.

4. Never compromise quality.

5. Build incrementally from firm foundations.

6. Develop iteratively.

7. Communicate continuously and clearly.

8. Demonstrate control.

The full detail of these principles can be found at www.dsdm.org. The rationale behind each principle is discussed further below.

7.1 Principle 1 – Focus on the business need

The overriding project goal is to deliver *what the business needs, at the right time and for the right price*. In order to fulfil this principle, DSDM Atern teams need to explore the true business priorities. MoSCoW prioritisation of requirements ensures that the Minimum Usable Subset to be delivered by the project is clear.

DSDM Atern roles incorporate the Business Sponsor, who owns the business case and understands the rationale for the project. They also include a Business Visionary, who carries the Business Sponsor's vision and objective for the project to the Solution Development Team on a continuous basis throughout the project. Business and end-user representatives, who understand how the project needs to support the specific business areas, work with the project throughout and are empowered to make decisions right through the project lifecycle.

These roles are fully described in Chapter 3.

7.2 Principle 2 – Deliver on time

Delivering on time is often critical for a project. Late delivery can undermine the business case, especially where market opportunities or legal deadlines are involved. Late delivery also consumes resources which may be needed for other projects. Resources being utilised beyond the dates that have been allowed for in the business case add to the cost and may invalidate the business case.

In order to fulfil this principle, DSDM Atern teams must Timebox the work and keep a clear focus on business priorities.

In order to achieve on time delivery, it actually helps if the Solution Development team establishes a reputation for timely and predictable deliveries. This way the people involved in the Timeboxes will *expect* their involvement to be needed at the times planned and will not be so inclined to double book their time in the belief that "these workshops never happen when the Project Manager says they will".

7.3 Principle 3 – Collaborate

Teams need to build a one-team culture between all stakeholders, and to actively cooperate and honour their commitments to each other. In order to fulfil this principle, DSDM Atern teams need to involve the right people and skills from a variety of disciplines throughout the project. They also need clear empowerment to take appropriate decisions within the team. Clear roles are defined to help with this. Facilitated Workshops enable stakeholders to share their knowledge effectively with other members of the project team. A collaborative and co-operative approach of all parties is needed. There are no winners on a failed project.

7.4 Principle 4 – Never compromise quality

In DSDM Atern, the level of quality to be delivered should be agreed at the start. A solution has to be fit for purpose: not over-engineered, but of the right level of quality to satisfy the business need. In order to fulfil this principle, DSDM Atern teams need to document and test appropriately and build in quality by constant review. Testing happens throughout the lifecycle. The motto is 'test as much as you can, as soon as you can': test early and continuously. Test-driven techniques may result in a test being written before the deliverable is actually produced. MoSCoW prioritisation and a risk-based approach are used to ensure that testing is appropriate.

7.5 Principle 5 – Build incrementally from firm foundations

This principle has two distinct aspects:

- Build in complete, small chunks (increments) in order to deliver real business benefit early;

- Build from firm foundations: establish sufficient understanding of the requirements and the solution space to mitigate risk.

DSDM Atern advocates incremental development, with Timeboxes focused on completed products. This encourages stakeholder confidence and promotes learning and improvement of the solution as increments are delivered and put into use. DSDM Atern teams will do just enough analysis and enough design up-front to create strong foundations, agreed by appropriate stakeholders, and strive for early delivery of business benefit. The acronym EDUF (enough design up front) is often used to signify this.

7.6 Principle 6 – Develop iteratively

Projects operate within a changing world. To attempt to lock this change out of a project will result in a solution which no longer meets the current needs. DSDM Atern allows for change during a project and uses Iterative Development to converge on an accurate business solution. In order to allow for change, DSDM works from a high-level statement of requirements and features, and only engages with the detailed requirements just in advance of building that particular element of the solution. It will then allow iteration, under control and within Timeboxes, so that the Atern teams can be creative, experiment, learn, and evolve a better solution. The concept of Iterative Development is embedded down to the lowest level of Timeboxing. The solution detail will evolve as the team learns more about it. User involvement allows the team to continually confirm that the correct solution is being built.

7.7 Principle 7 – Communicate continuously and clearly

Poor communication is often cited as the biggest single cause of project failure. DSDM Atern techniques are specifically designed to improve communication effectiveness for both teams and individuals. DSDM Atern teams use rich communication techniques, such as modelling and prototyping, to make early instances of the solution visible. They also use facilitated workshops to promote involvement and buy-in and manage stakeholder expectations throughout the project. Appropriate documentation is needed and this should be kept lean and timely. Informal face-to-face communication should be used where appropriate.

7.8 Principle 8 – Demonstrate control

In spite of its flexibility, an Atern project should not be out of control. It is essential to be able to demonstrate the status of the project at all times. A DSDM Atern team needs to be proactive when monitoring and controlling progress. In order to fulfil this principle, DSDM Atern teams should use an appropriate level of formality: make plans visible to appropriate stakeholders and measure progress through delivery of completed products rather than activities. The team will also evaluate continuing project viability based on the business objectives.

8. Success Factors and Project Risk

8.1 Factors Instrumental to Success (ISFs)

There are a number of factors that should be considered before embarking on the use of DSDM Atern for a particular project. Where these factors cannot be met, this constitutes a risk to the project. This does not mean that the use of DSDM is inappropriate for the project, but rather that the risk should be made visible and should form the basis for negotiation to improve the environment of the project.

For DSDM Atern to be successful there are a number of key elements that the organisation should have in place:

- *Acceptance of the DSDM Atern philosophy before starting work.* It is important that the Business Sponsor and senior management understand and accept the DSDM Atern philosophy. This includes acceptance of the meaning of MoSCoW prioritisation – that some features may be de-scoped, by agreement, in order to deliver on time and on budget.

- *Appropriate empowerment of the Solution Development Team.* Senior business management must either agree to delegate an appropriate level of decision-making to the Business Ambassador(s) in the Solution Development Team, or to take that role themselves. Similarly, the Solution Developers in the team should also be empowered to make appropriate technical decisions. Progress will be significantly hampered if the team has to wait for operational decisions to be made elsewhere. Empowerment is not unbounded and some decisions will still need to be escalated to more senior management. However, this should be the exception, and the majority of day-to-day decisions should be within the remit of the team.

- *Commitment of senior business management to provide the necessary Business Ambassador and Business Advisor involvement.* Business commitment and participation are absolutely critical. If this commitment is not achieved, the success of the DSDM Atern approach will be compromised.

- *Incremental delivery.* In order to gain an early return on investment, and to reduce risk, the organisation needs to be amenable to the incremental delivery of solutions. This applies to both business and development sides of the project. For instance, the business areas will need to handle incremental system growth, retraining, etc. and the solution developers will need good configuration management and release procedures that will not impede the process of delivery.

- *Easy access by Solution Developers to business roles.* Ideally the developers and business representatives will be co-located in their own dedicated environment, free from daily interruptions. However, this ideal may not be possible, and is not essential so long as contact is continual and frequent throughout the project.

- *Solution Development Team stability.* The overlapping development skills required (i.e. strong interaction throughout between Business representatives and Solution Developers) are vital to the speed of development, and the project will be put at risk if staff are swapped in and out. Specialists can be called in as required to support a team, but Solution Development Teams should remain stable.

- *Solution Development Team skills.* The team(s) must encompass the right skills in terms of both the business area and the technical environment. This does not mean that everybody needs to be a multi-skilled expert but that all the core skills for the project should be present in the team. All team members should demonstrate good interpersonal skills and be prepared to work collaboratively.

- *Solution Development Team size.* Each DSDM Atern team within the project should be small in order to minimise the overheads of management and communication, whilst optimising ownership. DSDM Atern recommends small teams, typically seven (plus or minus two) core members per team. The team headcount includes both Solution Developers and Business representatives. One project can have many DSDM Atern teams.

The Solution Development Team comprises the roles of: Team Leader, Business Ambassador(s), Business Analyst, Solution Developer(s) and Solution Tester. One project may have more than one Solution Development Team. Not everyone in the project will be within the Solution Development Team.

- *A supportive commercial relationship.* Where the supplier and customer are from different organisations and the development is covered by formal contract, or where Solution Developers are from the same organisation but working within a defined service level agreement, the relationship must accommodate the evolution of the system's requirements, without imposing onerous change management overheads on the evolving work of the Solution Development Team.

Summary of DSDM Atern?

Atern is an Agile Project Delivery Framework that delivers the right solution at the right time.

The right business solution is delivered because:
- The Project Team and other significant stakeholders remain focused on the business outcome
- Delivery is on time providing an early return on investment and reduced risk
- All people involved with the project work collaboratively to deliver the optimum solution
- Work is prioritised according to business need and the ability of users to accommodate changes
- Atern does not compromise quality

© TCC

8.2 The Project Approach Questionnaire (PAQ)

The Project Approach Questionnaire, shown in Figure 1.1, consists of a set of criteria for helping to determine the risks that need to be addressed when applying the DSDM Atern approach.

DSDM Atern Project Approach Questionnaire		Indicate the closest collective opinion					Where appropriate, comment on issues or risks related to a more negative response to this aspect of the DSDM Atern approach
Ref	Statement	Strongly Agree	Agree	Neutral	Disagree	Strongly Disagree	
1	The business driver behind the project is clearly stated and is visible to all members of the project team.						
2	The Business Sponsor and/or Business Visionary demonstrate clear ownership of the project.						
3	'The Business Sponsor, Business Visionary and Technical Coordinator all understand and accept the DSDM Atern philosophy.						
4	'The development has a clearly-defined timescale						
5	The requirements can be prioritised and there is flexibility to accept that not all requirements are 'Must Have' requirements.						
6	Requirements have been defined at a high level at the outset of the project, and it is acknowledged that changes are likely during development of the detail.						
7	It is accepted that the detail of both the requirements and the solution will emerge as the project progresses.						

8	The Business Sponsor and Business Visionary are aware of the importance of active business involvement and have the willingness and authority to commit appropriate business resources to the project as required.						
9	The Business Ambassadors are sufficiently empowered to guide the day to day evolution of the solution.						
10	The Solution Developers are sufficiently empowered to provide the best solution they can from a business perspective within pre-agreed architectural constraints.						
11	Solution development resources are allocated at an appropriate level and the team will be largely stable throughout the project (or, at least, throughout each increment).						
12	The Project Team and Solution Development team are able to adopt the roles and responsibilities within DSDM Atern.						
13	It will be possible for the Solution Developers to have easy access to Business Ambassadors and Business Advisors throughout the project.						
14	The Solution Development team (including both business and solution development resources) will have the appropriate collective knowledge and/or technical skills to deliver the solution.						
15	The Solution Development team (including both business and solution development resources) will have the appropriate soft skills (communication, negotiation etc.) to work effectively with each other and those around them.						
16	Strategies for continuous communication and collaborative working practices are sufficient to clearly support iterative development of the solution.						
17	The development technology tools and techniques support an iterative approach to solution development.						
18	There are no technical, contractual or other constraints to prevent the solution being broken into increments for development and delivery (even if the products of such increments are not deployed immediately).						
19	All project participants understand and accept that on-time delivery of an acceptable solution is the primary measure of success for the project.						
20	All parties accept that continual assessment of the fitness for purposes of all deliverables during development is essential.						
21	There are no mandatory standards or practices in force that will work against the evolution of a solution from a baselined set of high level requirements.						

Figure 1.1 The Project Approach Questionnaire

The questions in the PAQ are based on the DSDM Atern ISFs, the eight DSDM Atern principles and other project situational factors. The questions are intended for guidance only. They are a good set of criteria to have in place at the start of any project. As the experience of using DSDM Atern grows within an organisation, the list should be refined and expanded to fit with local constraints and practices.

It is not necessary to be able to provide a positive response to each of the questions. A negative response does not necessarily mean that the project cannot be run using DSDM Atern – rather it identifies a risk to be managed, a negotiation to be undertaken in order to improve the situation and to begin the project with less risk.

On completion of the PAQ, the DSDM Atern Practitioner or Atern Coach will be able to advise on whether the project under consideration should run under full DSDM Atern and, if not, which techniques are appropriate to the project.

The PAQ should be kept in view and managed alongside other risks throughout the project.

8.3 Project risk

Project risk relates to the threats posed to the project delivering on time, within budget and with the features required to the right quality. Ensuring that the DSDM Atern principles are respected significantly reduces project risk. There are two aspects to managing project risk:

- Recognise the risk;

- Handle the risk. This may mean the establishment of contingency plans to enact if the risk happens; insurance to transfer the cost if the risk materialises; measures to reduce or remove the risk; active acceptance that the risk is present but that nothing needs to be done about it.

Most procurers of projects are concerned with two risks: that the solution will not meet the needs of the business and that the project will overrun on time and/or cost. DSDM Atern is designed to mitigate both of these risks. Solutions that meet the needs of the business are delivered through the incremental and iterative approach with its continuous feedback from users. Cost and time overruns are avoided by the effective use of Timeboxes. Initially, the focus for mitigating risk will be on the DSDM Atern principles and the consequences of the project not meeting those principles.

9. Conclusion

We have seen the overall philosophy of DSDM Atern and how this is underpinned by eight principles. We have looked at the factors instrumental to success (ISFs) for a DSDM Atern project and considered these in line with risk.

Unlike some approaches, DSDM Atern fixes time and cost, and expects flexibility of the delivered features to maintain this. It uses MoSCoW prioritisation to identify the minimum usable subset of features to meet the business need; the lower priority features are also part of the plan, but provide the contingency to keep the project on track, within the control of clear team roles and clear product-based Timeboxes.

The involvement throughout the project of the right business representation and a clear focus on business need predisposes the DSDM Atern project to being successful.

Approach and Principles

1. **Which of the following statements is true?**

    A} DSDM Atern is a waterfall project management framework

    B} DSDM Atern is a modelling technique

    C} DSDM Atern is an agile project delivery framework

    D} DSDM Atern is an estimating framework

2. **DSDM Atern recommends:**

    A} Big design up front

    B} No design up front

    C} Just enough design up front

    D} Design from the front

3. **A benefit of using DSDM Atern is...**

    A} Project management is not needed since teams are self-organising

    B} Users are more likely to claim ownership of the solution

    C} Deployment can be done without technical help

    D} If the wrong system is built, the users only have themselves to blame

4. **What does DSDM Atern state about change?**

    A} Users always change their minds, so DSDM Atern needs to prevent change

    B} DSDM Atern avoids change whenever possible, because it causes problems

    C} Change is inevitable, so estimating should not be attempted

    D} DSDM Atern allows for change and harnesses its benefits

5. **The DSDM Atern philosophy is that:**

    A} Any project must be aligned to detailed technical goals

    B} Any project must be aligned to clearly defined strategic goals

    C} It is impossible to define what goals a project should align to

    D} Every project will change the strategic goals of the organisation

Answers can be found on page 222

Dynamic Systems Development
Method

Approach and Principles

© TCC   DSATP/1/ 1

Session Objectives

- What is Atern?

- Why have Atern?

- The philosophy and principles of Atern

- When to use Atern

© TCC   DSATP/1/ 2

**DSDM Atern is an
"Agile" Approach**

Exercise: What is Agile?

In groups:

Write down your top 5 words to describe "Agile".

© TCC   DSATP/1/ 3

What is DSDM Atern?

An Agile Project Delivery Framework that delivers the right
solution at the right time

- Any kind of project
- Focused on business benefit
- On time and in budget
- Quality and rigour
- Incremental
- Collaborative

© TCC   DSATP/1/ 4

The Agile Manifesto

We are uncovering better ways of developing
software by doing it and helping others do it.
Through this work we have come to value:

Individuals and interactions over processes and tools
Working software over comprehensive documentation
Customer collaboration over contract negotiation
Responding to change over following a plan

That is, while there is value in the items on
the right, **we value the items on the left more**

www.agilemanifesto.org
(2001)   DSATP/1/ 5

© TCC

DSDM - the History

- 1994/5 Dynamic Systems Development Method
  (DSDM) was written as a Framework for Business
  Centred Development

- Focus on delivering on time and in budget

- Focus on keeping quality

- It brought together best practices from the combined
  experience of DSDM Consortium members, including
  many "blue-chip" companies

- It was vendor-independent and became a standard,
  worldwide

© TCC   DSATP/1/ 6

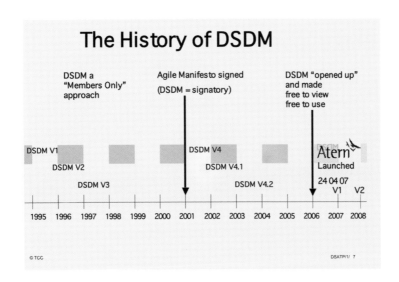

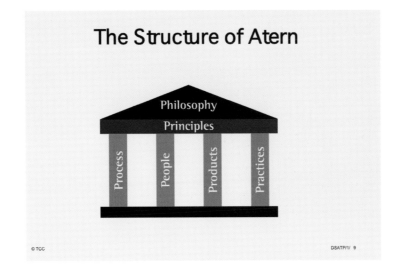

The Philosophy of Atern

Any project ...

- Must be aligned to clearly defined strategic goals
- Must focus upon early delivery of real benefits to the business

DSATP/1/ 10

The Philosophy of Atern

This is best achieved when key stakeholders ...

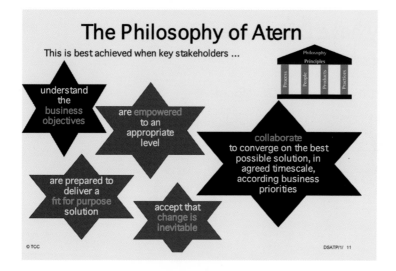

DSATP/1/ 11

... Not just software!

DSATP/1/ 12

The Benefits of Atern

- User ownership of the system is more likely

- Reduced risk of building the wrong system

- The final system is more likely to meet the users' real business requirements

- Users will be better trained

- Deployment is more likely to go smoothly

© TCC   DSATP/1/ 13

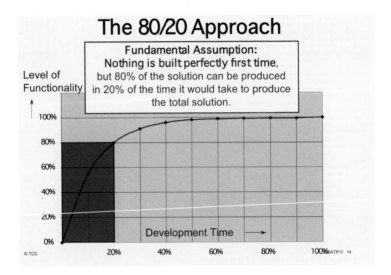

The 80/20 Approach

Fundamental Assumption:
Nothing is built perfectly first time,
but 80% of the solution can be produced
in 20% of the time it would take to produce
the total solution.

Level of Functionality

100%
80%
60%
40%
20%
0%

Development Time →

20%   40%   60%   80%   100%

© TCC   DSATP/1/ 14

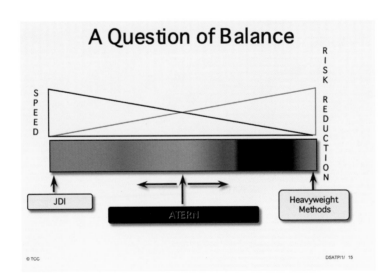

A Question of Balance

SPEED

RISK REDUCTION

JDI

ATERN

Heavyweight Methods

© TCC   DSATP/1/ 15

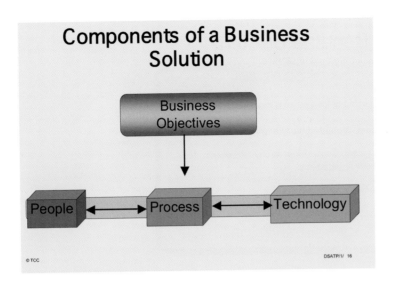

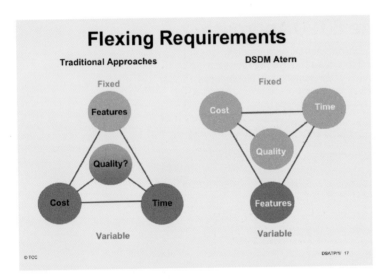

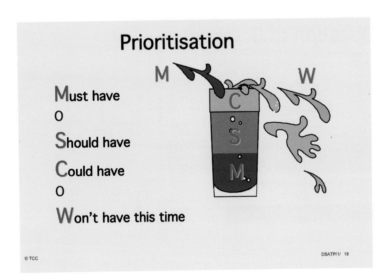

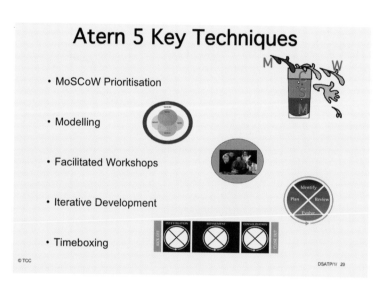

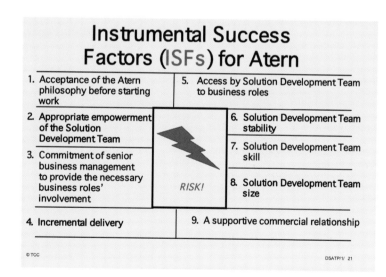

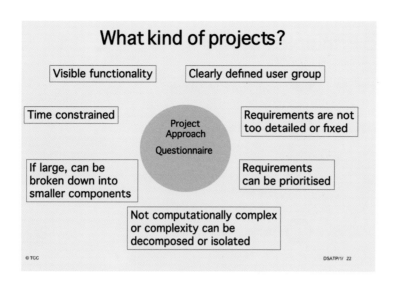

What kind of projects?

Visible functionality

Clearly defined user group

Time constrained

Project Approach Questionnaire

Requirements are not too detailed or fixed

If large, can be broken down into smaller components

Requirements can be prioritised

Not computationally complex or complexity can be decomposed or isolated

© TCC

DSATP/1/ 22

Summary of DSDM Atern?

Atern is an Agile Project Delivery Framework that delivers the right solution at the right time.

The right business solution is delivered because:
- The Project Team and other significant stakeholders remain focused on the business outcome
- Delivery is on time providing an early return on investment and reduced risk
- All people involved with the project work collaboratively to deliver the optimum solution
- Work is prioritised according to business need and the ability of users to accommodate changes
- Atern does not compromise quality

© TCC

DSATP/1/ 23

Session Summary

- What is Atern?
- Why have Atern?
- The philosophy and principles of Atern
- When to use Atern

© TCC

DSATP/1/ 24

Questions?

DSATP/1/ 25

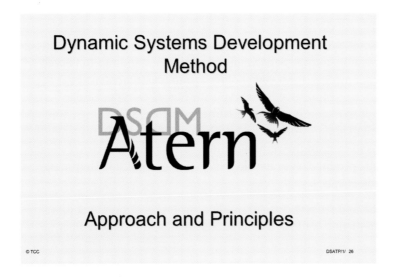

Dynamic Systems Development Method

DSDM Atern

Approach and Principles

DSATP/1/ 26

2

Modelling

1. Introduction

One of the main sources of errors and failures in projects is cited as the lack of good communication and the consequential misunderstandings between different stakeholder groups. Each stakeholder group (customers, users, managers, developers, technical experts) typically has its own particular jargon, which can lead to confusion and misinterpretation. Modelling, iterative development and prototyping are techniques designed to improve communications and prompt the right questions. They provide an early means of checking that the product being developed is what is required. They are a valuable aid to project success.

Many industries benefit from the use of models, prototypes and mock ups to establish requirements, confirm expectations and test the achievability of objectives. These can be as different as:

- A storyboard to represent a television advertisement;

- Architectural blueprints to define a housing development;

- An artist's impression of a landscaped park;

- A scale model of a car to be built;

- Process diagrams to establish the required functionality of software.

For example, in a software-related project, diagrams may be drawn to establish processes and their inter-relationships; later, screens may be presented, with no functionality, in order to check understanding of the requirement; these screens may then be refined and agreed with representatives of those who will use them. The screens may become the real screens of the final product, with logic being built behind them to make them function.

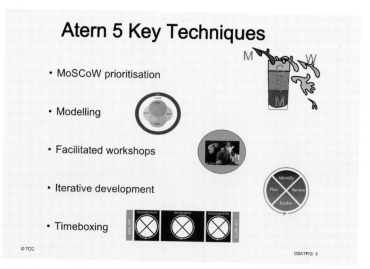

This chapter focuses on the modelling and in particular the early, diagramming aspects of modelling. Chapter 8 focuses on iterative development of the evolving solution, and the prototyping inherent in that process.

2. What is a Model?

A model can be defined as:

- A description or analogy used to help visualise something that cannot be directly observed;

- A small but exact copy of something;

- A pattern or figure of something to be made.

Models may be physical (a built version of some part of an eventual solution, a prototype: for example, working software) or may be expressed in a language: for example, a diagramming convention, with its own rules and symbols.

One of the DSDM Atern Principles specifically advocates communicating continuously and clearly, using 'rich communication'. In other words, many types of communication should be used, with a focus on the right type of communication for the target audience, arriving at the right time in the project, in a format and style that can be understood.

Models and diagrams are an approach to making elements of the product *visible* as early as possible but remember that the amount of time and effort put into a model should only be enough to satisfy the purpose of the model.

Modelling

A model is:

- A description or analogy (to help visualise something that cannot be directly observed)

- A small but exact copy of something

- A pattern or figure of something to be made

Many industries use models (and prototypes) to:
- Establish requirements
- Confirm expectations
- Test the achievability of objectives

Examples of models:
- Storyboards
- Diagrams
- Scale models (prototypes)
- Working software (prototypes)

2.1 Modelling and abstraction

Modelling usually incorporates some degree of abstraction, which involves omitting certain details from the model to allow clearer focus on another particular aspect.

For example, the map of the Metro system in a city shows just what it needs to, in order to communicate specific information to its target audience (the traveller). Its aim is to allow travellers to move from Station A to Station B. To do this, it shows just the stations and the links between them. It omits the power cables, the mechanisms to change tracks and the signals followed by the driver. It also does not show distances between stations – it does not need to convey this information to achieve its aim.

Another diagram, for a different purpose and target audience may actually show these other features.

It is essential when communicating in any form to answer the questions:

- Who is it for?

- What do they need it for?

2.2 Modelling and prototyping

Modelling and prototyping are linked concepts. A prototype is always a kind of model; a model is not necessarily a prototype. For example, we can model an *existing* situation: a building; a staffing structure; a database structure. A prototype usually implies a *new* structure.

In information systems projects and software engineering, the term *model* has traditionally been used to refer to a set of diagrams.

These may be formulated in a defined language, such as the Unified Modelling Language (UML). UML is an open method used to specify, visualise, construct and document the artefacts of a software-intensive development project. UML offers a standard way to create a system's *blueprints*, including components such as:

- The people involved with the product (actors);

- The processes;

- The data;

- The locations where the product will be operated.

Using UML, diagrams can help to gain an understanding of the features required, and then to assist in the creation of other artefacts, such as programs. The programs are working prototypes which, when refined and tested, will evolve into the eventual solution.

2.3 Target audience for the model

A model is information on something (content, meaning), that is:

- Created by someone (sender);

- For someone (receiver);

- For some purpose (usage context).

It is important that the level of detail and the language used is appropriate for the target audience of the model. In DSDM Atern, models are used to communicate between teams of mixed specialisms (users, technologists, solution developers). It is vital that the effectiveness of any particular modelling approach to these different receivers is considered.

2.4 The viewpoints for modelling

A coherent picture of a solution area can be gained by considering the perspectives: what, where, when, how, who and why, and the relationships between them. For example: who performs which processes; what data is needed to support each process. Matrices can be helpful in drawing these relationships.

Table 2.1 below shows an interpretation of these perspectives from a software-related point of view, but parallels can easily be drawn for other types of project.

WHAT	The information within the solution area, data, relationships and business rules.
HOW	The functions, features and processes within the solution area.
WHERE	The locations at which the business operates, in relation to the solution area.
WHO	The people: customers, users, stakeholders.
WHEN	The events of importance to the business (times and scheduling).
WHY	The business objectives and strategy, as related to the project.

Table 2.1 Perspectives used in modelling

DSDM Atern does not advocate the drawing of models from all of these perspectives, unless it is useful to do so. However, it is worth checking during a project whether any perspective has been missed rather than intentionally omitted.

2.5 Modelling from a single user-role perspective

Rather than model the entire business area at once, it is often better to focus on (and model) the aspects of the product needed for a particular user role to carry out a specific task. This approach is likely to achieve individual user buy-in since they can readily see the purpose. It will ensure that each user is able to focus on areas which are of most interest to themselves, and in which they have the most knowledge and experience to contribute.

This user-centred (task-based) view cuts across the above perspectives, providing the answer to all six questions for a specific user responding to a specific business event.

3. Modelling in the DSDM Atern Lifecycle

The level of modelling at each phase of the DSDM Atern lifecycle must be appropriate to the level of complexity and characteristics of the project/ programme in question.

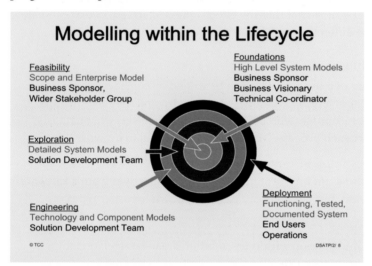

3.1 Pre-Project

In the Pre-Project phase, the organisation's strategic planners and possibly programme managers have identified an opportunity or need and are considering setting up a project to address this. The project owner will be identified and brief Terms of Reference will be laid out, sufficient to obtain agreement to start the project. The definition of 'why' (business objectives and rationale for the idea) forms the Terms of Reference for the project. At this point, models from a previous solution in the same business area may be a useful short-cut to understanding the problem and clarifying the objective. A very rough prototype of the initial ideas may help stakeholders to understand what is being proposed.

3.2 Feasibility

In Feasibility, the Feasibility Assessment needs to provide a high-level overview of the project from a business and technical perspective, with an Outline Business Case, an Outline Solution and a Feasibility Prototype. Communication is with the organisation's strategic planners, the project owner and key stakeholders. The levels of models required at this point are usually a simple 'big picture' to convey scope and the essence of what is being planned. This could incorporate models of the current situation in addition to models of proposed solution options. Initial clarity and a shared vision are paramount and will guide the rest of the project. A Feasibility Prototype is often produced at this time, to illustrate a solution or to perform a Proof of Concept test. The Outline Solution could include diagrams and/or working prototypes to convey the different options being considered.

3.3 Foundations

In Foundations, a firm starting point is established from Business, Solution and Management perspectives. The team is beginning to work in more detail on the definition and prioritisation of the requirements. Modelling from the perspectives of what, where, when, how, who, why is useful here. High level solution models will be sufficient to understand dependencies and to estimate well enough for laying out the Delivery Plan for the first increment. Models will also communicate the scope of the system and highlight areas out of scope. High level models will be used to analyse the whole breadth of the solution space, to communicate ideas and to identify inconsistencies, dependencies and omissions. End-to-end diagrams of the solution will also be useful. The current situation could also be modelled – such models drawn here will be invaluable as an aid in the Deployment phase.

Solution options may result in several sets of high level models. These may be from a logical or conceptual perspective (showing what is proposed, but deliberately omitting how, when, where and who). Later models will show different technical options, taking in the physical perspectives of how, when, where and who. A Solution Prototype may also be constructed here, often as a disposable prototype. The why perspective will look at the requirements, and may diagram the links between these, together with links to project and business objectives.

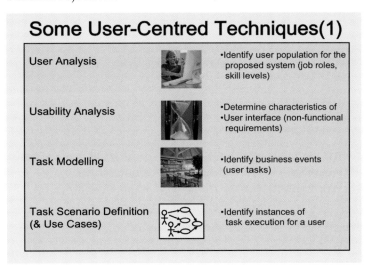

3.4 Exploration

During Exploration, the Business Model, Design Model and Prototype Solutions may be used to help to analyse the solution in detail, to communicate ideas and to further analyse increments of the solution. Both end-to-end diagrams and single-user perspectives may be useful here. Models will be high level models of the big picture plus incrementally delivered detailed models as each increment is undertaken.

3.5 Engineering

In Engineering, the full technical detail for solution developers must be presented clearly. What, where, when, how, who, why are all relevant perspectives to model from. Models here are used to inform the construction of the solution, and as such may need to be technical, precise and detailed. The solution will be prototyped and the Deployable Solution will be, effectively, the final working prototype, once tested. With DSDM Atern there will usually be many increments to be deployed, and therefore many elements of the models which will emerge, evolving from previous models.

3.6 Deployment

In Deployment, component models of the existing situation will be useful along with detailed models of the Deployable Solution and models from the user perspectives of how the solution will be used. These should link users to the elements of the solution that are related to them, thereby easing deployment planning. The Deployed Solution is the working, implemented version of the final prototype, and non-implementable models, such as diagrams, can provide user and support/maintenance documentation.

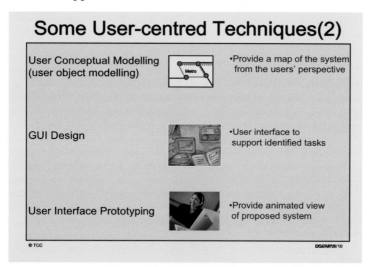

3.7 Post-Project

In Post-Project, the models used to analyse and understand the system are useful to document and support the system.

It should be emphasised here that the above phases are not serial: Exploration, Engineering and Deployment may overlap significantly in iterative development and deployment. Also, none of the models are mandatory, but should be used when they are an aid to understanding and to identifying dependencies and structure of the solution area.

There is a transition here from the 'as is' models of the current situation to the 'to be' models which represent the solution elements. It is necessary to distinguish between these and clearly show which is being modelled, to avoid confusion later. It is also usually advisable not to excessively document the 'as is' situation unless, for example, it needs to be detailed to support business change initiatives. The Business Visionary and Business Ambassador roles are embodiments of such information and should be available throughout the project, which limits the amount of excessive detail which sometimes obscures such models and reduces their effectiveness.

Modelling Tips

- Level of overhead

- Easily understood by user and developer

- Support process of serial refinement

- Models produced must enhance communication

- Must lie easily within the Atern framework

© TCC   DSATP/2/ 11

4   Conclusion

Whatever the product or business solution being developed, DSDM Atern recommends an iterative, incremental and collaborative approach, following the DSDM Atern Lifecycle. This approach places a high demand on communication:

- DSDM Atern advocates clear and continuous communication, using rich communication techniques, of which the development of models is a key element. These should be developed iteratively, taking a top-down approach to detail and modelling from different perspectives;

- Models should always be an aid and not a bureaucratic overhead;

- There should always be a clear focus on addressing the intended audience for the models, using models which they will understand;

- There must always be emphasis on using models to enhance the effectiveness of communication for all members and levels of the development process;

- The use of models, and the formality with which they are created and reviewed, will depend on the nature of the project and on the skills and experience of the team. The models for the building of a new power station, with its safety-critical nature, will necessarily be more detailed, complex and more formally reviewed than those for the building of a small website;

- DSDM Atern does not limit itself to particular modelling techniques, although there are some industry-standards. In a software development project, UML, user stories, architectural spikes and class models may all be used. The simplest rules are to do what works for the project and the organisation; capitalise on the skills which exist within the organisation; use diagrams and models to establish a common language between the teams; do enough modelling and no more;

- Models should be used to see the overall picture at a high level, and then to help to break down the project into comprehensible chunks that are easier to manage than the whole and can be handled incrementally. Modelling is to help people to visualise complex things. In DSDM Atern, they can then be used as a basis for increment and Timebox planning;

- The intention is always the development of a working solution, or part of the solution, as soon as possible. However, an appropriate amount of design up-front, and a few well chosen models and prototypes throughout can save the cost of expensive mistakes.

Modelling

1. **Modelling is a key technique in DSDM Atern for which of the following:**

   A} Improving collaboration and communication

   B} Avoiding the production of documents

   C} Definition of the lowest level of detail as early as possible in the lifecycle

   D} A welcome break from e-mails

2. **What does DSDM Atern define as a simple rule for modelling?**

   A} Do enough and no more so that the purpose of the model is achieved

   B} Do enough and no more until Deployment

   C} Do significant detail by the end of Foundations

   D} Do a thorough, fully-detailed design up front, using models

3. **In DSDM Atern, the 'Why' viewpoint for modelling refers to...**

   A} The objective and requirements

   B} Whether the project is agreed

   C} The locations excluded from the project

   D} The reasons for 'Won't Have' requirements being left out.

4. **In DSDM Atern, a model refers to:**

   A} Only the finished product of the project, once it has been deployed

   B} A cardboard cut-out of the final product

   C} A representation of some or all of the issues in the project

   D} A diagram, picture or prototype representing some or all of a product

5. **In DSDM Atern, the modelling viewpoint 'When' refers to:**

   A} The events of importance to the business

   B} The final project deadline

   C} The functional requirements

   D} The certainty of delivery of Must Haves

Answers can be found on page 222

Dynamic Systems Development Method

Atern

Modelling

Session Objectives

- What is modelling

- Modelling perspectives

- Modelling within the lifecycle

- Modelling tips

Atern 5 Key Techniques

- MoSCoW prioritisation

- Modelling

- Facilitated workshops

- Iterative development

- Timeboxing

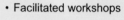

Modelling

A model is often a diagram:

Group Exercise
What diagrams do you know / use in a development project?

Modelling

A model is:

- A description or analogy (to help visualise something that cannot be directly observed)

- A small but exact copy of something

- A pattern or figure of something to be made

Many industries use models (and prototypes) to:
- Establish requirements
- Confirm expectations
- Test the achievability of objectives

Examples of models:
- Storyboards
- Diagrams
- Scale models (prototypes)
- Working software (prototypes)

Modelling

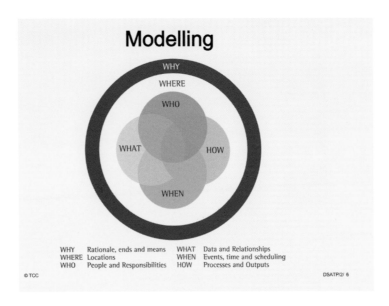

WHY	Rationale, ends and means	WHAT	Data and Relationships
WHERE	Locations	WHEN	Events, time and scheduling
WHO	People and Responsibilities	HOW	Processes and Outputs

© TCC

DSATP/2/ 6

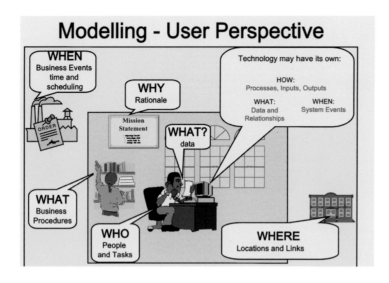

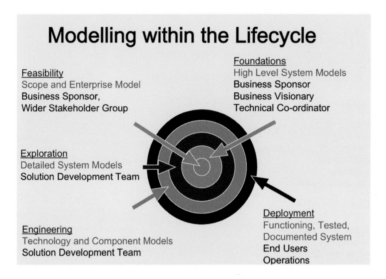

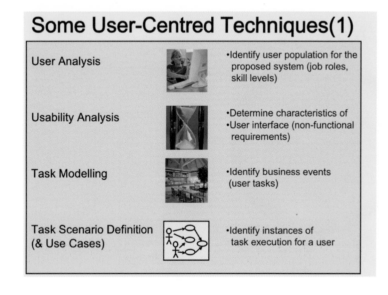

Some User-centred Techniques(2)

User Conceptual Modelling (user object modelling)		•Provide a map of the system from the users' perspective
GUI Design		•User interface to support identified tasks
User Interface Prototyping		•Provide animated view of proposed system

Modelling Tips

- Level of overhead

- Easily understood by user and developer

- Support process of serial refinement

- Models produced must enhance communication

- Must lie easily within the Atern framework

Session Summary

- What is modelling

- Modelling perspectives

- Modelling within the lifecycle

- Modelling tips

Dynamic Systems Development Method

Modelling

© TCC   DSATP/2/ 13

3. Roles, Skills and Team Structures

1. Introduction

One of the major factors in the success of any project is the people who are involved. It is therefore imperative that the DSDM Atern team is organised in an effective way. Managing Atern projects relies on the Project Manager focusing, motivating and supporting their empowered teams, rather than micro-managing at a task level. For this to work, the team must take on their empowerment and be self-directed and self-organising. However, a degree of clarity of roles and responsibilities saves confusion and wasted time.

This session covers the major people issues which affect the outcome of a DSDM Atern project, including:

- The team structure;

- The roles and responsibilities;

- The empowerment of the team;

- The essential skills of the team.

2. DSDM Atern Teams – Self-Directed Teams

DSDM Atern projects are dynamic, with rapidly evolving solutions and continuous involvement of business roles. DSDM Atern teams consist of a cross-functional mix of technical, development and business representatives working together. DSDM Atern teams need to be self-directed and self-organising, rather than wait to be 'tasked' by a Project Manager. They need to take responsibility, and accept accountability, for completing work. Table 3.1 below compares typical DSDM Atern self-directed team behaviour with the behaviour of a more traditional, tightly managed team:

Tightly managed teams	Self-directed teams (DSDM Atern)
Take directions	Take initiative
Seek individual reward	Focus on team contributions
Focus on low-level objectives	Concentrate on solutions
Compete	Co-operate
Comply with processes, regardless of outcome	Continually look for better ways of working
React to emergencies	Take steps to prevent emergencies

Table 3.1 Comparison of tightly managed teams and DSDM Atern teams

In a traditional project, a signed-off specification of expected functions and features is often used in a defensive way by the solution developers, to point out to business representatives that 'it isn't in the specification and therefore we didn't agree to do that'. The result of this is that either the business does not get the functionality rendered in a way which is useful, or that extra money has to be paid for the necessary functionality to be introduced. Either way, the relationship between the business and the solution developers is damaged, with blame being cast.

DSDM Atern advocates a 'no-blame' policy and joint responsibility in the development – a true partnership, where the Solution Development Team, made up of business and development representatives with equal responsibility for the eventual product, work together to achieve the best product possible for the business within the time and cost constraints. It is essential that the individuals within the team do identify and accept their responsibilities. However, if problems develop, the team must work together towards team success, rather than being satisfied to identify an individual's failure and to cast blame.

DSDM Atern teams have a number of defined roles, some of which must be assigned to team members from the business, some to solution developers and some which could be assigned to either. It should be noted, however, that it is possible for one individual to be assigned to more than one role, and that some roles may be split between two or more people, where this makes sense.

Composition of the team depends on both personalities and skills. Experience has shown that small teams work best, and the aim is to keep team size to no larger than nine (Miller's limit of seven plus or minus two applies here). This means that on a large project, the recommended approach is the division of the products into small manageable chunks, which can then be allocated to small Solution Development Teams: this mirrors small craft teams working on small complete pieces of the product, rather than a factory production line approach to product development. The Project Manager should give consideration to what mix of team personalities and skills will be effective and should always be prepared to change the structure if the team is not working well together.

3. DSDM Atern Roles and Skills

People working together effectively are the foundation of any successful project. DSDM Atern recognises this and assigns clear roles and responsibilities to each person in a project, from all perspectives of the project. The different skills represented in the team must work very closely together, with no 'us and them' attitudes. It is understood that such things as geographical constraints and staff availability can impact the setting up of the ideal team, but it is strongly recommended that the roles are all considered and their individual responsibilities assigned as appropriate. Roles and responsibilities defined by DSDM Atern can be used as the basis for personal Terms of Reference for the project.

The key roles in DSDM Atern are divided into the following three categories:

Project level roles

These are the managers, coordinators and directors of the project work. They are not normally involved in the day-to-day development of the solution, although they should always have sufficient visibility of it to understand progress and provide strategic direction from a business, technical or project governance perspective, as required. The project level roles are:

- Business Sponsor;
- Business Visionary;
- Project Manager;
- Technical Coordinator.

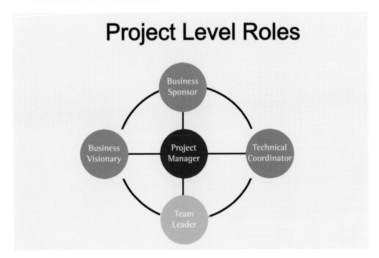

Solution Development Team roles

These are the shapers and builders of the solution. They are collectively responsible for the day-to-day development of the solution and for assuring its fitness for business purpose. The Solution Development Team roles are:

- Team Leader;
- Business Ambassador;
- Business Analyst;
- Solution Developer;
- Solution Tester.

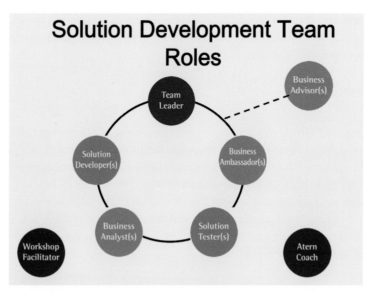

Other roles

These cover other stakeholders, perspectives and specialisms not specifically defined above, but which may need to be represented during some projects. These roles provide assistance and guidance to the project team as required during the lifecycle. They include:

- Business Advisors;

- Workshop Facilitator;

- Atern Coach;

- Specialists.

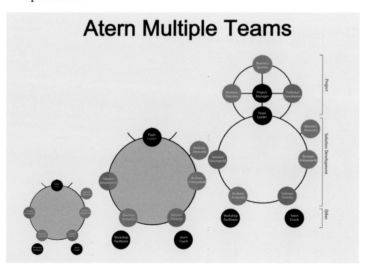

3.1   Business Sponsor

This is the most senior project level business role. The Business Sponsor is the project champion who is committed to the project, the proposed solution and the approach to delivering it. Specifically responsible for the Business Case throughout (however formally or informally this may be expressed), the Business Sponsor will own the solution once delivered and will be responsible for the realisation of any benefits associated with it.

The Business Sponsor must hold a sufficiently senior position in the organisation to be able to resolve business issues (e.g. to force open closed doors) and make financial decisions. This role has a crucial responsibility to ensure and enable fast progress throughout the duration of the project.

There should be only one person responsible for this role within a project. This person should be committed and available for the duration of the project, providing a clear escalation route.

Responsibilities:

- Owning the Business Case for the project;

- Ensuring ongoing viability of the project in line with the Business Case;

- Ensuring that funds and other resources are made available as needed;

- Ensuring the decision making process for escalated project issues is effective and rapid;

- Responding rapidly to escalated issues.

3.2 Business Visionary

This is a senior project-level business role. More actively involved than the Business Sponsor, the Business Visionary is responsible for interpreting the needs of the Business Sponsor, communicating these to the team and, where appropriate, ensuring they are properly represented in the Business Case. The Business Visionary remains involved throughout the project, providing the team with strategic direction and ensuring that the solution delivered will enable the benefits described in the Business Case to be achieved.

The Business Visionary role ensures the project's coherence and fitness for purpose from the business perspective (the Technical Co-ordinator performs the same function from the technical perspective).

Responsibilities:

- Owning the wider implications of any business change from an organisational perspective;

- Defining the business vision for the project;

- Communicating and promoting the business vision to all interested parties;

- Monitoring progress of the project in line with the business vision;

- Contributing to key requirements, design and review sessions;

- Approving changes to the high-level requirements in the Prioritised Requirements List;

- Ensuring collaboration across stakeholder business areas;

- Ensuring business resources are available as needed;

- Promoting the translation of the business vision into working practice;

- Acting as the arbiter of disagreements between team members on the interpretation of requirements.

3.3 Project Manager

The Project Manager role is a project-level role responsible for all aspects of the delivery of the solution. As well as providing high-level management direction to the project team(s), the role is focused on managing the working environment in which the solution is evolving. The Project Manager co-ordinates all aspects of management of the project at a high-level; however, in line with the Atern concept of empowerment, the Project Manager is expected to leave the detailed planning of the actual delivery of the product(s) to the Team Leader and members of the Solution Development Team.

Although the Project Manager role is delivery-focused, this does not dictate from where in an organisation the role is resourced. Appropriate sourcing of the role will depend on the skills and knowledge required.

It is vital that the Project Manager takes responsibility throughout the duration of the project. This must include both business and technical delivery aspects of the project, from establishing the Feasibility and Foundations of the project, through to the Deployment of the solution.

Responsibilities:

- Communicating with senior management and the project governance authorities (Business Sponsor, Project Board, Steering Committee etc.) with the frequency and formality that they deem necessary;

- High-level project planning and scheduling, but not detailed task planning;

- Monitoring progress against the baselined project plans;

- Managing risk and any issues as they arise, escalating to senior business or technical roles as required;

- Managing the overall configuration of the project;

- Motivating the teams to meet their objectives;

- Managing business involvement within the Solution Development Teams;

- Resourcing specialist roles as required;

- Handling problems escalated from the Solution Development Teams;

- Coaching the Solution Development Teams when handling difficult situations.

3.4 Technical Co-ordinator

As the project's technical design authority, the Technical Co-ordinator ensures that the Solution Development Teams work in a consistent way, that the project is technically coherent and meets the desired technical quality standards. The role provides the glue that holds the project together, whilst advising on technical decisions and innovation.

The Technical Co-ordinator performs the same function, from a technical perspective, as the Business Visionary does from a business perspective.

Responsibilities:

- Agreeing and controlling the technical architecture;

- Determining the technical environments;

- Advising on and co-ordinating each team's technical activities;

- Identifying and owning architectural and other technically-based risk, escalating to the Project Manager as appropriate;

- Ensuring the non-functional requirements are achievable and subsequently met;

- Ensuring adherence to appropriate standards of technical best practice;

- Controlling the technical configuration of the solution;

- Managing technical aspects of the transition of the solution into live use;

- Resolving technical differences between technical team members.

3.5 Team Leader

Reporting to the Project Manager, the Team Leader ensures that a Solution Development Team functions as a whole and meets its objectives. The Team Leader works with the team to plan and co-ordinate all aspects of product delivery at the detailed level. This is a leadership role rather than a management role and the person holding it will ideally be elected by his or her peers as the best person to lead them through a particular stage of the project. It is therefore likely that they will also perform another Solution Development Team role (e.g. Business Analyst, Solution Developer or Solution Tester) in addition to their team leadership responsibilities. It is also feasible that the person carrying out the Team Leader role could be different from one Timebox to another, where the Timeboxes have a different focus.

Responsibilities:
- Focusing the team to ensure an on-time delivery of the agreed products;

- Encouraging full participation of team members within their defined roles and responsibilities;

- Ensuring that the iterative development process is properly focused and controlled;

- Ensuring that all testing and review activity is properly scheduled and carried out;

- Managing risks and issues at the Development Timebox level, escalating to the Project Manager or Technical Coordinator as required;

- Monitoring progress on a day-to-day basis for all team activities;

- Reporting progress to the Project Manager;

- Running the short daily team meetings, ensuring they are timely, focused and brief.

3.6 Business Ambassador

This is a business role within the Solution Development Team. The Business Ambassador generally comes from the business area being addressed and provides business-related information from the perspective of those who will ultimately make direct use of the envisioned solution. The role provides the business perspective for all decisions related to the way the solution's fitness for business purpose is defined and implemented.

Working closely with the rest of the Solution Development Team, the Business Ambassador guides the evolution of the solution, bringing other users' input and ideas to the project as required. As a true ambassador, the role is responsible for the day-to-day communication channels between the project and the business. The Business Ambassador must have the desire, *authority*, responsibility and knowledge to be able to ensure that the right solution emerges in order to meet the business need. This does not necessarily imply a senior position within the organisation, but *a level of empowerment* during the project to fulfil the role and an allocation of time to fully participate in the project as required.

Responsibilities:

- Contributing to all requirements, design and review sessions;

- Providing the business perspective for all day-to-day project decisions;

- Providing the detail of business scenarios to help define and test the solution;

- Communicating with other users, involving them as necessary and getting their agreement;

- Providing day-to-day assurance that the solution is evolving correctly;

- Organising and controlling business acceptance testing of the solution;

- Developing business user documentation for the ultimate solution;

- Ensuring user training is adequately carried out;

- Attending the short daily team meetings (daily stand-ups).

3.7 Business Analyst

The Business Analyst is fully integrated with the Solution Development Team and focuses on the relationship between the business and technical roles, ensuring accurate and decisive direction is provided to the Solution Development Team on a day-to-day basis. The Business Analyst ensures that the business needs are properly analysed and are correctly reflected in the guidance the team needs to generate the envisioned solution.

Active involvement of the business users in the process of evolving the solution is vital to the success of a DSDM Atern project. So it is important to ensure that the Business Analyst does not become an intermediary *between* the Solution Developers and the Business Ambassadors and Business Advisors, but rather supports and facilitates the communication between them.

Responsibilities:
- Ensuring all communication between business and technical participants in the project is unambiguous and timely;

- Managing development, distribution and baseline approval of all documentation and products related to business requirements and their interpretation;

- Ensuring that the business implications of all day-to-day decisions are properly thought through.

3.8 Solution Developer

The Solution Developer interprets business requirements and translates them into a deployable solution that meets functional and non-functional needs. Many different specialist skills may need to be represented here. Additionally, the Solution Developer needs to be a good listener and communicator, because of the collaborative nature of working on a DSDM Atern project, and they should also have an appreciation of the business area of the solution, in order to make clear communication possible. A person fulfilling this role should ideally be allocated full-time to the project. If this is not the case, it introduces significant risk to the project's Timeboxing approach.

Responsibilities:
- Working with business roles and Solution Testers to iteratively develop:

- The deployable solution;

- Models required for the properly controlled development of the solution;

- Models and documentation required for the purpose of supporting the solution in live use.

- Recording (and later interpreting) the detail of any:

    - Changes to the detailed requirements;

    - Changes to the interpretation of requirements which result in re-work within the solution;

    - Information likely to impact on the ongoing evolution of the solution.

- Adhering to technical constraints laid out in the Solution Architecture Definition;

- Adhering to standards and best practice laid out in the Technical Implementation Standards;

- Participating in any quality assurance work required to ensure the delivered products are truly fit for purpose;

- Testing the output of their own work prior to independent testing.

3.9 Solution Tester

The Solution Tester is fully integrated with the Solution Development Team and performs testing in accordance with the Technical Testing Strategy throughout the project. The Business Ambassador role is responsible for all user testing, but may be assisted by the Solution Tester, as part of the team, since the Solution Tester will have specialist testing skills not always held by the Business Ambassador.

Responsibilities:
- Working with business roles to define test scenarios and test cases for the evolving solution in accordance with the Technical Testing Strategy;

- Carrying out all types of technical testing of the solution as a whole;

- Creating testing products (e.g. test cases, plans and logs);

- Reporting the results of testing activities to the Technical Coordinator for Quality Assurance purposes;

- Keeping the Team Leader informed of the results of testing activities;

- Assisting the Business Ambassador(s) and Business Advisor(s) to ensure that they can plan and carry out their tests well enough to make sure that the important areas are covered.

3.10 Business Advisor

Often a peer of the Business Ambassador, the Business Advisor is called upon to provide specific and often specialist input to solution development or solution testing. The Business Advisor will normally be an intended user or beneficiary of the solution but may, for example, simply provide legal or regulatory advice with which the solution must comply.

Responsibilities:
Based on the specialism for which the Business Advisor has been engaged:

- Providing specialist input into relevant:

    - Requirements, design and review activities;

    - Day-to-day project decisions;

    - Business scenarios to help define and test the solution.

- Providing specialist advice on, or help with:

    - Organising and controlling business acceptance testing of the solution;

    - Developing business user documentation for the ultimate solution;

    - User training.

3.11 Workshop Facilitator

The Workshop Facilitator is responsible for managing the workshop process and is the catalyst for preparation and communication. The Workshop Facilitator is responsible for the context of the workshop, not the content.

The Workshop Facilitator should be independent of the outcome to be achieved in the workshop.

Responsibilities:
For each workshop:

- Agreeing the scope of the workshop with the workshop owner;

- Planning the workshop;

- Familiarisation with the subject area of the workshop.

Engaging with participants to:

- Confirm their suitability as a participant (in terms of knowledge and state of empowerment);

- Ensure their full understanding of the workshop objectives;

- Understand any major areas of interest and concern in the subject area;

- Encourage completion of any required preparation work;

- Facilitating the workshop to meet its objectives;

- Reviewing the workshop against its objectives.

3.12 DSDM Atern Coach

The role of the DSDM Atern Coach is there to help a team with limited experience of using Atern to get the most out of the approach within the context of the wider organisation in which they work. The DSDM Atern Coach should ideally be independently certified in Atern to ensure competency in this role.

As with any method of working in any context, the approach cannot be followed blindly. If there is something in the project environment that will inhibit the effectiveness of a particular Atern technique, then it is vital that the potential problem is addressed. Typically, there are two ways of addressing such a problem: the first is to influence the environment to allow the technique to be effective; the second is to adapt or substitute the technique. Either way, an expert in the DSDM Atern process – the Atern Coach – will have the knowledge and experience to help.

Responsibilities:

- Providing detailed knowledge and experience of DSDM Atern to inexperienced DSDM Atern teams;

- Tailoring the DSDM Atern process to suit the individual needs of the project and the environment in which the project is operating;

- Helping the team use DSDM Atern techniques and practices and assisting those outside the team to appreciate the DSDM Atern philosophy and value set;

- Helping the team work in the collaborative and cooperative way demanded by DSDM Atern and other Agile approaches;

- Building DSDM Atern capability within the team.

3.13 Specialist Roles

The Solution Development Team roles will not cover every skill that needs to be involved in a project.

Specialist Roles

Specialists may be brought in as required:
- Business consultants
- Technical consultants
- Specialist in human factors
- Configuration manager
- Quality manager
- Systems integrator
- Operations co-ordinator
- Support and maintenance specialists
                              and many others ...!

Specialist roles may need to be brought into the Solution Development Teams on an ad hoc basis to fulfil specific functions. The required roles will depend on the size and nature of the project. Some examples of specialist roles are:

- Trainers, to facilitate skills transfer;

- Business advisors with particular specialist business knowledge (subject matter experts – SMEs);

- Implementers, to support the transition of products to a live environment.

The required specialist input to the Solution Development Team should be formally planned, the individuals identified and their availability checked so that they can attend relevant meetings, facilitated workshops, etc. Their responsibilities should be defined so that they clearly understand their role and what is expected of them.

It is also possible to have specialist roles at the *Project Level.* At this level, the specialist involvement is less likely to be ad-hoc, and would more commonly be throughout the project. A common example of a project level specialist role would be an Operations Co-ordinator, who is responsible for the operational aspects, both during design and implementation, and who also ensures that any new solution is included in Disaster Recovery Planning, Capacity Planning and Availability Planning.

Atern Roles & Responsibilities

Project level roles:
- Business Sponsor
- Business Visionary
- Project Manager
- Technical Coordinator

Solution Development Team roles:
- Team Leader
- Business Ambassador
- Business Analyst
- Solution Developer
- Solution Tester

Other roles include:
- Business Advisor
- Workshop Facilitator
- Atern Coach
- Specialist

Some examples of specialist roles are given in Table 3.2, but the list is by no means exhaustive and will vary with the project, and the industry in which it is operating.

Specialist role	Responsibility
Business Consultant	An expert (internal or external) in a particular business field to offer advice and guidance or to produce a document.
Business Process Co-ordinator	To promote, develop and co-ordinate the new or changed business processes.
Capacity/Performance Planner	To advise on capacity requirements for the final solution; to advise on any performance requirements.
Compliance Specialist	To advise on legal, data protection, audit trail and any other compliance aspects.
Corporate Risk	To advise on and assist in the management of risk to the business either through delivery of, or without the solution.
Environmental Advisor	To advise on the implications for the natural environment either through delivery of, or without the solution.
Human Factors Specialist	To advise on the design of the user interface.
Industrial Relations	To manage relationships and agreements between staff and management.
Infrastructure Provider	To provide and set up the hardware, system software and communications environment required for both development and production.
Operations Co-ordinator	It is necessary to involve the people who will be responsible for the operational aspects of the solution, to ensure that the new system is ready to be included in the operational environment, alongside other already established systems and services, and is included in any Disaster Recovery Plans.

Quality Manager	As required by the organisation's quality management system.
Security Specialist	To advise on any security requirements.
Service/Help Desk Manager	To advise and negotiate the Service Level Agreement for support and to agree how the system will be handled by the Service Desk.
Technical Consultants	A technical expert (internal or external) to provide expertise in specific areas such as networking, operational considerations, tools usage, technical reviews.
Training Provider	To provide training in use of the solution.

Table 3.2 Examples of specialist roles in DSDM Atern

NOTE: Although not a specifically-defined role in DSDM Atern, there is often a need for the role of *Scribe* to be covered. The role requires someone who is a good listener/communicator, with good written communication skills who understands the project jargon.

A Scribe role within team meetings, prototyping sessions and demonstrations should have business and technical awareness to keep the necessary records of requirements, agreements, decisions reached. An approach quite often taken on projects is to rotate the role between team members in other roles.

A Scribe role within Facilitated Workshops is often used to support the Facilitator, and may even have the strength of being a Co-Facilitator. The Workshop Scribe role may also be taken by many different people during the life of a project.

4. Conclusion

To operate successfully, a DSDM Atern Team should be self-directed and highly motivated. The team should be made up of people from the business and technical areas, all carrying equal responsibility for the success of the end product, within a team success culture where problems are team problems, not a cause for laying blame.

The team should consist of good communicators. They should hold regular (daily but short) informal but planned team meetings. It is also helpful if team members can be physically co-located, although it is accepted that this may not always be possible. It is the responsibility of the Project Manager to enable an effective environment and means of communication for the team, whether or not they are co-located.

Appropriate, consistent business involvement is essential and can only be assured if the Business Sponsor secures co-operation of other business managers and if the business managers are prepared to release staff for significant periods of time, even full-time if needed.

Roles, Skills and Team Structures

1. **Which of the following statements is true?**

   A} In DSDM Atern, one person must always hold one, and only one, role

   B} In DSDM Atern, one person can hold more than one role

   C} In DSDM Atern, one person must always hold several roles

   D} In DSDM Atern, none of the roles can be split between two people

2. **In a DSDM Atern team, the Business Ambassadors are:**

   A} Occasional visitors to the team

   B} A great help if they can spare the time

   C} Responsible full members of the team

   D} Only required at the end of Engineering, for User Acceptance Testing

3. **In DSDM Atern, the business roles include Business Ambassador and:**

   A} Workshop Facilitator

   B} Technical Co-ordinator

   C} Business Solution Tester

   D} Business Visionary

4. **Which role is responsible for taking a wider view of the end-to-end business process?**

   A} Business Advisor

   B} Business Ambassador

   c) Business Sponsor

   D} Business Visionary

5. **Which of the following is a responsibility of the Project Manager?**

   A} Ensuring that funds and other resources are made available

   B} Promoting translation of the vision into working practice

   C} Managing risk and handling escalated problems

   D} Planning workshops

Answers can be found on page 222

Dynamic Systems Development Method

Atern

Roles, Skills and Team Structures

Session Objectives

- How do Teams Work?

- Team Size and Style

- Atern Roles and Responsibilities

How do Teams work?

Group Exercise

DSDM Teams

- self-directed
- small
- composed of users and developers with equal responsibility

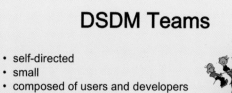

- subject to re-structuring if team is not working

- underpinned by a team success approach/no blame culture

Atern Roles & Responsibilities

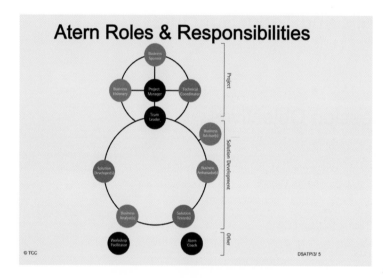

© TCC

DSATP/3/ 5

Project Level Roles

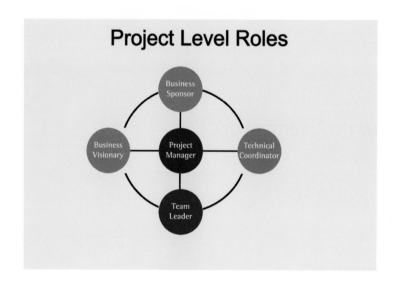

The DSDM Atern Student Workbook | **Chapter 3 – Roles, Skills and Team Structures**

Solution Development Team Roles

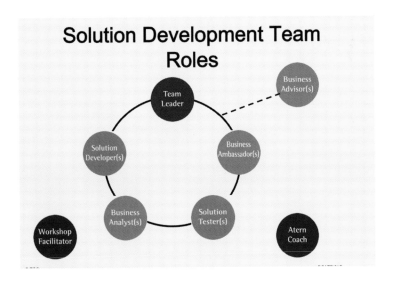

Atern Multiple Teams

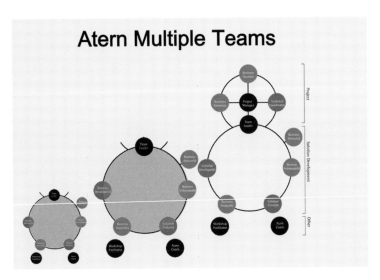

Specialist Roles

Specialists may be brought in as required:
- business consultants
- technical consultants
- specialist in human factors
- configuration manager
- quality manager
- systems integrator
- operations co-ordinator
- support & maintenance specialists
  and many others ...!

4. Lifecycle and Products

1. Introduction

DSDM Atern defines a configurable lifecycle which should be tailored to suit individual projects. The lifecycle is designed to allow frequent product delivery, iterative and incremental development, active business involvement, interwoven testing and early delivery of business benefits.

A business area may be the subject of many projects throughout its life. DSDM Atern considers the whole development lifecycle of a business solution as well as the lifecycle of any particular project in relation to that overall solution. There are activities which happen before and after any particular project. There are seven phases in the DSDM Atern lifecycle:

FIVE main phases:

- Feasibility;
- Foundations;
- Exploration;
- Engineering;
- Deployment.

Plus TWO further phases:

- Pre-Project;
- Post-Project.

Each is defined in terms of:

- Objectives;
- Preconditions;
- Points to consider.

The phases are described further in the remainder of this chapter.

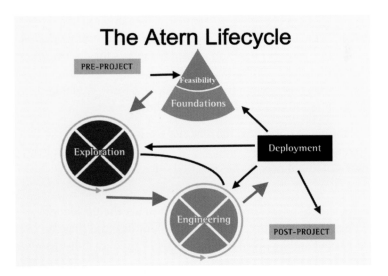

2. The Pre-Project Phase

Projects need to be set up correctly from the outset to ensure success. The work of the Pre-Project phase formalises a proposal for a project, clarifies the project objective and places it in the context of other potential work to be, or already being, carried out by the organisation.

Projects may stand alone or may exist as part of a programme or portfolio of several projects, often with a shared business change objective.

2.1 Objective

- To describe the business problem to be addressed;
- To identify a Business Sponsor and Business Visionary;
- To confirm that the project is in line with business strategy;
- To produce terms of reference for the project;
- To scope, plan and resource the Feasibility phase.

2.2 Preconditions

A project has been proposed.

2.3 Points to consider

The work of the Pre-Project phase should be short: usually all that is needed is a brief statement justifying the start up of a project's Feasibility phase and outlining the business need and expected scope.

Projects are initiated in many different ways that determine which Pre-Project activities are appropriate. These include:

- Clarifying the need for the project;
- Linking the project to business and/or IT strategic planning;
- Allocating initial budget for Feasibility and checking resource availability.

If the project is part of a programme, budget will already have been allocated, the Business Case approved and strategy alignment will have been checked. Thus, little or nothing remains to be done Pre-Project other than allocate resources and a timeframe for Feasibility.

If the project is a stand-alone piece of work, mandated by someone in a position of power within the organisation, a considerable amount of work may need to be done in the Pre-Project phase: obtaining resources for the Feasibility and outline agreement that there would be resources allocated thereafter. Many projects waver in the early stages, when the right people are not available. They may lose credibility and buy-in from both customer and supplier.

For organisations planning to outsource most of the work of a project, the Pre-Project work is often done before a decision is made on a particular supplier. This means that much of it will need to be revisited once the contract has been awarded.

The Pre-Project work should be minimal; just enough to get the project off the ground and to ensure that resources are agreed in outline, and that the key stakeholders are identified and involved from the start of the Feasibility Study.

3. Feasibility Phase

The Feasibility phase provides the first opportunity for agreeing whether a proposed project is viable from both business and technical perspectives, by means of a high level investigation of the potential solutions, costs, benefits, risks and timeframes.

The Feasibility phase seeks to confirm an Outline Business Case for the project and an Outline Plan. Various options for the technical solution will be considered and timescales and costs will be estimated. The system scope will be outlined, the problem which the system must address will be clarified and the chosen technical and business options will be defined, with a recommended way forward.

The Feasibility phase should only go to the level of detail required to assess whether a feasible solution exists and to select the most appropriate one. The detail of the requirements, risks, plans and costs for the solution, outlined here, will be developed in the later phases.

3.1 Objectives

- To establish whether there is a feasible solution to the business problem described in the Terms of Reference;
- To identify the benefits expected/needed from the delivery of the proposed solution;
- To outline possible approaches for delivery, including solution sourcing and project management approach;
- To describe the organisation and governance aspects of the project;
- To state first cut estimates of timescale and costs for the project;
- To plan and agree resources for the Foundations phase;
- To produce a Feasibility Assessment and an Outline Plan for the project.

3.2 Preconditions

- The Terms of Reference for the project has been approved;
- The required resources are available to carry out the Feasibility phase;

- The Business Sponsor and Business Visionary have sufficient time available to help shape the project.

3.3 Points to consider

The Feasibility phase should be kept as short as possible; its only purpose is to establish the viability of the project and the approach to be used, and to provide enough information to justify progressing to the Foundations phase. The detail of the investigation happens in the Foundations phase.

If a project is not viable, it is important that work on it is halted as early as possible, to minimise waste of money and resources.

If the project is small and simple, it is acceptable to merge this phase with the Foundations phase.

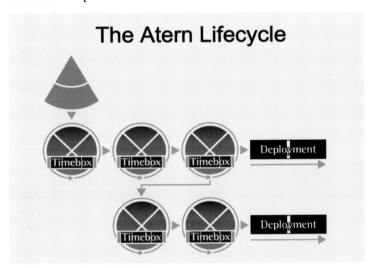

4. Foundations

The Foundations phase is aimed at establishing a clear start (firm foundations) for the project. In establishing the foundations, the three essential perspectives of business, solution and management need to be combined to provide a clear project focus that is both robust and flexible.

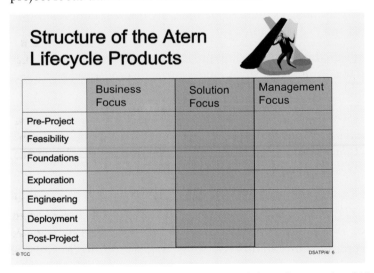

Detail, particularly around the specifics of the solution, should be strictly limited so that it does not unnecessarily constrain the way the solution evolves, but still clearly demonstrates that it will be able to meet the needs of the business. For the description of the solution, although outline technical solutions will be proposed, the focus is more strongly on 'what' than 'how'.

4.1 Objectives

- To agree and baseline the high level requirements for the project, their respective priorities (MoSCoW) and relevance to the business need;
- To describe the high level business processes to be supported by the proposed solution (where appropriate);
- To identify at a high level the structure of information used, created and updated by the proposed solution (where appropriate);
- To outline and agree strategies for solution deployment;
- To develop a sufficient Business Case to direct and focus the project;
- To establish an outline of the solution architecture and identify the physical or infrastructural elements of the solution;
- To define technical implementation standards;
- To describe how quality will be assured;
- To establish appropriate governance and organisation for the rest of the project;
- To describe the solution development lifecycle for the project along with techniques to be applied in managing the project and for demonstrating and communicating progress;
- To agree and baseline a schedule for development and deployment activities for the solution;
- To record, assess and manage risk associated with the project.

4.2 Preconditions

Agreement of the Feasibility Assessment and Outline Plan.

4.3 Points to consider

Significant business input will be required during the Foundations phase. The relevant business representatives must be identified early and their level of involvement agreed and budgeted for.

Technical input will also be needed, to input to the business-need focused prioritisation, and to ensure that any planning is correctly sequenced and estimates are sensible

A time limit for the Foundations phase should be set. This is not an easy phase to rigidly Timebox, as there is less flexibility of elements which can be de-scoped to stay on time. However, having a visible Timebox will focus the work of Foundations.

The aim of this phase is to create a high level, but sound, view of the business and technical aspects of the project. The justification for the project must be assessed and a clear decision taken to continue with the work beyond this phase; stopping a project at this point, because of a fragile business case (too risky, too costly, low benefits), should be considered a successful outcome of the Foundations phase.

The Project Manager and the Technical Coordinator are respectively responsible for setting up appropriate levels of management and technical control for the project during the Foundations phase.

5. Exploration

The Exploration phase is used to evolve, in complete product chunks, the detail of the business requirements and to translate them into a form which can be developed, during the Engineering phase, into a viable solution.

The end product of Exploration will be refined further during the Engineering phase to ensure a deployable product which functions as required, including the meeting of acceptance criteria for non-functional aspects such as performance, security and maintainability.

5.1 Objectives

- To evolve the detail of the requirements, which have been agreed and baselined in the Prioritised Requirements List, in an incremental and iterative way;

- To evolve and define a functional solution that demonstrably meets the needs of the business;

- To give the wider organisation an early view of the solution that they will eventually operate, support and maintain;

- To evolve the products of the Foundations phase into models that make visible the structure of the intended solution and its support for the impacted business areas.

5.2 Preconditions

- The Foundations products have been accepted and provide an adequate foundation for the project, from which a solution can evolve;

- The appropriate physical and technical environments are in place to support the evolution of the solution;

- All required project personnel and stakeholders are engaged as required.

5.3 Points to consider

The approach to planning the development of the evolving solution is flexible; Exploration and Engineering phases may be interwoven, overlap or be merged. The intent is to take feature-based chunks of the Prioritised Requirements List and aim to deliver working increments of the eventual solution as early as practicable. This allows the DSDM Atern team to deliver real business value early, and also to gain feedback from early deployments to inform and improve later increments of the evolving solution.

6. Engineering

The Engineering phase is used iteratively and incrementally to evolve the products of Exploration to achieve full operational readiness.

The continued involvement from the business representatives during this phase provides an ongoing opportunity to validate fitness for business purpose from functional and non-functional perspectives.

6.1 Objectives

- To refine the evolving solution from the Exploration phase to meet the agreed acceptance criteria;

- To expand and refine any products required to successfully operate and support the solution in live operation.

6.2 Preconditions

- The Business Visionary has acknowledged that the functionality demonstrated in the evolving solution from Exploration is in line with the vision for the final business solution;

- The appropriate physical and technical environments are in place and adequately set up to support the evolution of the solution;

- All required project personnel and stakeholders are engaged.

6.3 Points to consider

The Exploration and Engineering aspects of the DSDM Atern framework are highly configurable; these phases may overlap considerably.

Testing is undertaken throughout the DSDM Atern lifecycle, and during both Exploration and Engineering a Tester role is present within the Solution Development Team.

A Deployment Plan is produced during Exploration and Engineering. By the end of the Engineering phase, for each increment, there should be a fully developed Deployment Plan to define the schedule for deployment and to allow a smooth transition of the project's products into operational use. A Benefits Realisation Plan is also a part of this.

7. Deployment

The primary purpose of the Deployment phase is to move the solution into live use. Where the end product of the project is to be sold or distributed outside of the organisation creating it, the Deployment phase is used to ensure that the product is fully complete and ready to sell. Deployment also provides a key review point for the project.

The number of passes through the Deployment phase will depend on how many separate increments of the overall solution are planned to be delivered.

7.1 Objectives

- To install or release the solution (or increment) into the live business environment;

- To provide necessary documentation to support the live operation of the solution in the business environment and, where applicable, to train the end users of the solution;

- To provide documentation for operations and support staff who will be responsible for supporting and maintaining the solution and, where applicable, to train operations and support staff;

- To assess whether the deployed solution is likely to deliver the intended elements of business benefit described in the Business Case;

- After each increment:
    - To confirm the ongoing performance and viability of the project and re-plan as required.
- After the final deployment:
    - To formally bring the project to a close;
    - To review overall project performance from a technical and/or process perspective;
    - To review overall project performance from a business perspective.

7.2 Preconditions

The deployable solution has been approved for deployment.

The live environment is ready to receive it.

7.3 Points to consider

If the solution is being deployed incrementally, it is usually appropriate to formally assess whether the project should continue after each incremental deployment. It is possible, because of the business-value prioritisation of the deliveries within a project, that the vast majority of the benefits might be enabled by early increments and that the value of later increments may be marginal. It makes sense, therefore, to check that investment in the rest of the planned project will provide a reasonable return. Justification to continue is likely to reflect the cost of operating the solution as it stands against the cost of operating a more complete solution.

8. Post-Project

The Post-Project phase takes place after the last planned deployment of the solution. Its purpose is to reflect on the performance of the project in terms of the business value actually achieved. This assessment should start as soon as the value can be measured, normally three to six months after the completion of the project.

8.1 Objectives

To assess whether the benefits expected from the project have actually materialised.

8.2 Preconditions

The solution has been deployed into the live, operational environment.

8.3 Points to consider

In many cases, the project will have been closed prior to the start of the Post-Project phase. In some projects where the overall solution is delivered incrementally, it is often appropriate to start the assessment of benefits before the final deployment. Under such circumstances, it may be appropriate and beneficial to feed ideas for change or enhancement back into the ongoing project.

The Business Sponsor and Business Visionary have an ongoing responsibility for ensuring that the benefits enabled by the project are actually realised through proper use of the solution provided.

9. Paths Through the Lifecycle

DSDM Atern's lifecycle offers options for all types of project and is very configurable.

DSDM Atern projects will usually have a Feasibility phase followed by a Foundations phase. When a project is assessed to be simple, low-risk and of short duration, these two phases may, optionally, be merged.

This early work is used to determine the best way to develop the required solution and this is where the subsequent path through the DSDM Atern lifecycle is determined.

Actual development work is typically divided into one or more increments, each normally marked by the deployment of an increment of the working solution into the live environment. Increments are in turn divided into development Timeboxes.

The focus of a development Timebox may reflect a single development phase (either Exploration or Engineering) or may be a combination of both.

9.1 Development cycles

Exploration and Engineering cycles each consist of four stages which make up a development cycle:

- *Identify* deliverables to be evolved;
- *Agree* plan for evolving deliverables;
- *Evolve* the deliverables;
- *Review* the deliverables.

Identify deliverables to be evolved
By prioritising the functional and non-functional requirements, those which are essential to be developed can be identified whilst those which are less important can be deferred. In this way the project is divided into possible deliverables in line with the solution areas offering greatest business benefit. The focus is also maintained by defining the acceptance criteria before development begins.

Agree plan for evolving deliverables
The timeframe for the development in a DSDM Atern project will not be allowed to 'slip' and although DSDM Atern embraces change as a natural part of the development process, if additional functions or features emerge that need to be incorporated, then choices have to be made about what will have to be left out to accommodate this within the timeframe.

Evolve the deliverables
A deliverable can be created in the early phases of a DSDM Atern project, and will involve significant time from business users and Solution Developers as they explore the business requirements. As the emphasis shifts to performance and other non-functional requirements, the bulk of the effort will be developer time, although business involvement is still required.

Review the deliverables
After development, deliverables have to be reviewed. The review also serves to confirm that the project is on-track as well as ensuring increased business ownership both in terms of what has been developed and the future direction

of the project. This building of ownership will make a significant contribution to the acceptance of the system when completed.

10. Conclusion

DSDM Atern defines a configurable lifecycle which can be tailored to suit the needs of individual projects. The lifecycle allows for frequent product delivery, iterative and incremental development, active business involvement, testing throughout and early delivery of business benefits. There are many paths through the lifecycle and each phase is defined in terms of objectives, pre-conditions, and points to consider.

Lifecycle and Products

1. **When is the viability of the project first assessed from a business and technical perspective?**

   A} Exploration

   B} Foundations

   C} Feasibility

   D} Engineering

2. **When are Feasibility and Foundations phases likely to be combined?**

   A} When the teams need to get into Exploration as soon as possible

   B} When the project is a rush job

   C} When a project is assessed as simple, low risk and of short duration

   D} When business time is limited

3. **The phases of the DSDM Atern lifecycle in between Pre-Project and Post-Project are:**

   A} Feasibility, Foundations, Exploration, Engineering, Deployment

   B} Feasibility, Foundations, Construction, Engineering, Deployment

   C} Feasibility, Foundations, Exploration, Construction, Deployment

   D} Feasibility, Foundations, Excavation, Engineering, Deployment

4. **Two phases of the DSDM Atern lifecycle which may be combined are:**

   A} Pre-Project and Post-Project

   B} Feasibility and Deployment

   C} Foundations and Exploration

   D} Exploration and Engineering

5. **What does DSDM Atern say about the paths through the lifecycle?**

   A} Atern's lifecycle offers options for all types of project

   B} Atern's lifecycle is fixed, although requirements may vary

   C} Atern's lifecycle is an optional part of the approach

   D} Atern has only one path through the lifecycle

Answers can be found on page 222

Session Objectives

- The lifecycle
- The phases
- The products

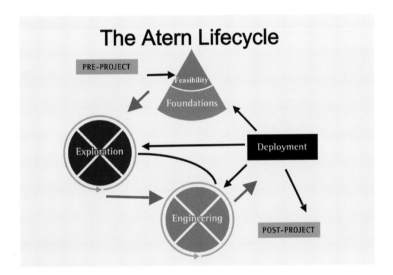

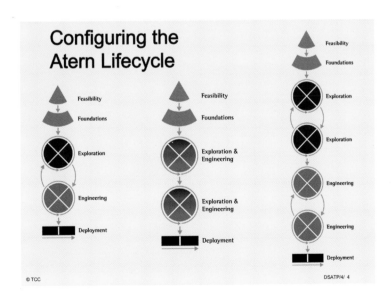

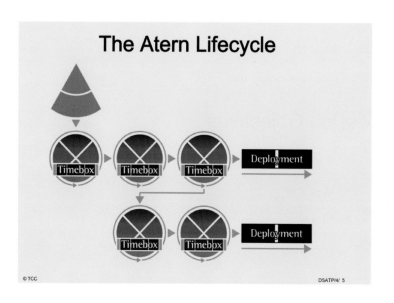

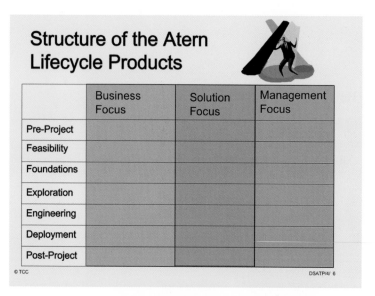

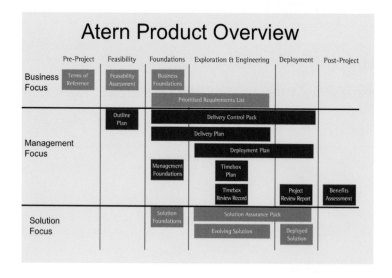

Session Objectives

- The lifecycle
- The phases
- The products

Dynamic Systems Development Method

The DSDM Atern Lifecycle

5. Project Management Considerations

1. Introduction

Project management within DSDM Atern has some fundamental differences from traditional project management. This chapter examines these differences and looks at some of the major issues of project management: risk, configuration management, quality and testing, metrics and maintainability.

Some of the issues that a project manager has to consider, such as team management structure and user involvement, have been discussed in earlier chapters. Others such as Timeboxing, planning and estimating will be discussed later.

2. Traditional versus DSDM Atern Project Management

Traditional project approaches are often focused upon delivering the functionality described in a fixed specification and on controlling resource levels, in an attempt to keep the project on schedule and within budget.

Management of traditional projects is about control, including the control of change to that fixed specification. Managing a DSDM Atern project is about recognising that change is a natural part of business projects; to exclude change may result in delivering a product which meets the original specification, true at the outset of the project, and not the current business need which is present as a result of changes that have occurred during the project lifespan. The DSDM Atern Project Manager's challenge is to enable constant change, if needed, whilst maintaining the target of a fixed delivery date for a usable, business-valuable solution.

Traditional v. Atern Project Management

Traditional:
- Strict adherence to specification
- Control of resource

...in order to hit time and budget for the fixed specification

Atern:
- Evolutionary change to specification
- Collaborative, 'no-blame' user/developer relationship
- Timeboxing

...to deliver a valuable element of the solution on time

DSDM Atern may require changes to organisational, social and technical elements of project culture. The collaboration in Atern projects requires a strong degree of trust and a 'no blame' culture. It is the responsibility of the Project Manager to ensure that collaboration is effective and that confrontational attitudes do not emerge between team members. The DSDM Atern Project Manager focuses on motivating and supporting the empowered Solution Development Teams, rather than micro-managing at a task level. Progress is demonstrated by delivery of completed, business-relevant products, rather than by production of progress reports. When significant problems do occur, it is also important for the Project Manager to have established the agreement of the Business Sponsor to a clear escalation process, to enable fast decision making.

In a DSDM Atern project, building the right system to meet the business need is of primary importance. The key to DSDM Atern project management is to maximise business benefit by delivering essential functionality within tight timescales through controlling how much is developed rather than extending the time allotted or allowing the quality to be compromised.

These objectives are achieved by:

- Iterative development and prototyping;

- Focusing on high priority features which will deliver maximum business benefit;

- Active business involvement;

- Empowerment of the team;

- Frequent delivery.

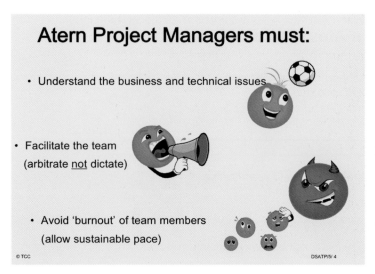

2.1 Sustaining team morale

The morale of a DSDM Atern team is usually sustained by the high rate of progress and the positive feedback from the business about the quality of the frequent deliverables. To avoid morale slipping when setbacks occur, it is important for the Project Manager to monitor the morale of the team and to build in or encourage frequent rewards and celebrations of success.

The DSDM Atern team must be genuinely empowered to make day-to-day decisions on the evolution of the solution, if speed of development and delivery are to be maintained. This tends to lead to a democratic environment, rather than a command-and-control one for the Project Manager. Project Managers accustomed to exercising strong personal control may initially find the management of a DSDM Atern project unsettling. A change of style and approach will be necessary, but the benefits in terms of end-product fit and business user satisfaction will be great.

Communication

- An environment conducive to good communication
- Team members who are good communicators
- Co-located teams, where possible
- Daily "Stand-ups"
- Facilitated workshops & retrospectives
- Modelling and prototyping

© TCC   DSATP/5/ 5

2.2 Setting team objectives

The Solution Development Team needs clear objectives, based on business products. The team should be empowered to achieve these objectives in its own way, rather than the Project Manager planning at task-level, in advance. For the approach to be successful the objectives must be measurable and the team should be involved in estimating and setting realistic objectives. It is the responsibility of the Project Manager to ensure that there is a clear understanding about what is to be delivered in each Development Timebox and to ensure that the relevant requirements are established in detail by the Solution Development Team. It is extremely likely that priorities and requirements will alter as the project progresses. It is only through accepting such change that the final solution can be assured to meet the business need. The Project Manager must be open to accepting such changes whilst ensuring that any consequences are fully understood by all concerned.

3. Project Management Considerations

The following topics will be covered here from a DSDM Atern project perspective:

- Control (and monitoring progress);

- Risk Management;

- Configuration Management;

- Quality;

- Testing;

- Metrics;

- Maintainability.

3.1 Control

In a traditionally-managed project, activities are monitored and controlled against a detailed plan. In a DSDM Atern project, there is still a plan. The DSDM Atern Delivery Plan is a Timeboxed plan, based on products rather than activities. The Solution Development Teams are empowered to organise their own activities from this, to achieve completion of the products within the Timeboxes. Products carry business priorities, based on the MoSCoW categories. The plan does not carry contingency for slippage; instead, it is kept on track by de-scoping, by agreement, the lower priority features.

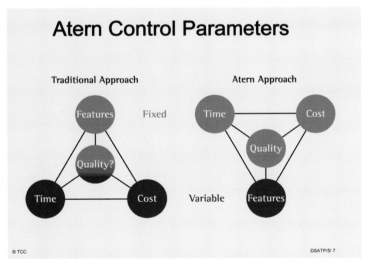

Much of the control in a DSDM Atern project emerges naturally from the structuring of a project with small teams and tight Timeboxes. Keeping plans visible at all times to all relevant team members and stakeholders is also vital in achieving control.

It is also important to capture information on the actual time spent delivering the products, in order to improve future estimating.

In DSDM Atern, progress is monitored through the delivery of completed products, unlike traditional approaches, which often attempt to track earned value on incomplete elements of work.

Within Timeboxes, techniques such as Burn Down charts and Burn Up charts are useful for visibly demonstrating the current status and the projected outcome. Simple progress charts (Kan Ban charts) showing the following can be used for detailed task planning within Timeboxes:

- Tasks to do;

- Tasks in progress;

- Tasks done.

Such progress charts are usually created by the team, but can be valuable to the Project Manager because they make the team's progress visible.

There are a number of valuable tools that aid both team and project communication and these are now described below:

Daily Stand-ups
The Daily Stand-up meeting is recommended as an informal, but planned, team communication.

This must be kept brief to be effective and, typically, will not exceed 15 minutes (about two minutes per team member). The Team Leader or Project Manager will usually facilitate the meeting, to keep it to time and ensure everyone remains focused on its format and purpose.

The meeting is open to anyone in the Atern project, but is intended as a Solution Development Team update from each team member. The format of the Daily Stand-up is for each team member to state:

- What they have done since yesterday's Stand-up;

- What they intend to do today;

- Any problems, risks, issues (and if any, who is needed to work with the team member to resolve these).

If during a Timebox, the team identifies an issue or risk that is obviously beyond the scope of the Timebox to handle, it needs to be escalated to the project level, with the agreement of the Project Manager.

Co-location
A small team located together can avoid the communication problems experienced by larger, geographically-separated teams. Wherever possible, projects should be subdivided on a business product basis, into small, self-sufficient, co-located teams.

Where this is not possible, and teams are necessarily large or are dispersed across a variety of locations and even time zones, technology to support rich and informal communication may be needed. This should be planned and enabled by the Project Manager early in the project.

Escalation route
When a situation develops in a project that makes the projected results difficult or impossible to achieve, escalation to higher levels of authority may be needed.

The necessary higher-level decision-makers then jointly determine whether or not to change the parameters of the project (usually time, scope or budget). In a DSDM Atern project, the Business Visionary's on-going involvement means that issues can often be resolved through discussion with them, rather than needing formal escalation. Additionally, the built-in scope flexibility of MoSCoW prioritisation gives room for bringing a project back on track, without compromising quality and without the need for formal escalation.

When escalation is needed, Table 5.1 shows the levels of decision making which apply to a DSDM Atern projects. (Where a DSDM Atern project is part of a multi-project programme, more levels may occur.)

Level	Decision topic and where defined
Steering	Project Scope (goals and high level results), time, budget, high-level resources, other management constraints. Defined in the Outline Plan, Management Foundations and Delivery Plan products.
Project	Approach, phasing, increments strategy, functional and non functional requirements on a high level, intermediate results, resources, technical architecture, technical guidelines. Defined in the Management and Solution Foundations products (including, where applicable, the Business Area Definition, System Architecture Definition and Development Approach Definition).
Team	Daily and weekly planning, decisions on who does what, low-level functional and non-functional requirements, the approach to delivering results. Embedded in Timebox Plans and various aspects of the Evolving Solution.

Table 5.1 Levels of decision making within a DSDM Atern project

When an escalation occurs, speed of decision making, empowerment and a cooperative and collaborative approach are essential. Each level has to decide whether it can resolve the issue within its own empowerment, rather than escalating. Once escalated, higher levels of management must be made aware that any delays impact upon deliverables; prior agreement of turn-around times for escalated issues will help. While the problem is being escalated, the team(s) involved should concentrate on consolidating results or on activities that are not influenced by the decision at hand. In this way, no time is wasted.

3.2 Risk Management

A project risk is defined in DSDM Atern as 'something that may happen and, if it does, will have a detrimental effect' on the outcome of the project.

Another popular definition of a risk is 'uncertainty of outcome' and this acknowledges both opportunity and threat. This is not incompatible with the DSDM Atern definition since even the opportunity, if not taken account of, can render a detrimental effect.

The purpose of Risk Management is to ensure that the risks facing a project are identified, assessed and managed.

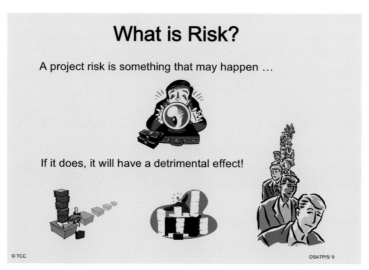

This includes:

- Identification of risks that may threaten the project for business, systems or technical reasons;

- Assessment of the impact of those risks on the success of the project should they arise. This assessment involves deciding on the likelihood of the risk occurring and, if it does, on the severity of its impact on the project;

- Management of those risks through planning specific countermeasures that are aimed at either avoiding the identified risks or accepting them and minimising their detrimental effect on the project, or applying the appropriate countermeasures when a risk materialises.

The risks established as a result of activities should be recorded in the Risk Log, which is part of the Delivery Control Pack, one of the management products of Foundations.

Where Atern Reduces Risk

- Traditional approaches use time contingency
- Agile NDUF, traditional BDUF

- Requirements unknowable up-front
- Requirements change

- Sign off

Using DSDM Atern to reduce risk
In the following common situations DSDM Atern can reduce risk:

- The business does not know exactly what it wants: DSDM Atern supports an evolving solution and emerging understanding. Techniques such as iterative development, modelling and prototyping allow the Solution Development Team to work together to agree the detail as the solution is evolving;

- The business change their minds about what is required: In a DSDM Atern project, change is accepted as inevitable. The low-level detail is not defined until the latest possible point. Also MoSCoW prioritisation allows new requirements to be incorporated without extending the project timeframe;

- Not all detail can be agreed at the start: DSDM Atern advocates doing Enough Design Up Front (EDUF), not too much, not too little. This should be sufficient to allow the project to progress safely without all detail being defined at the outset;

- The business is unwilling to commit to a final sign-off: The products of the project emerge incrementally, avoiding the risk involved with one large sign-off. The business has been represented throughout the evolution of the product to be signed-off, and understands first-hand the detail that the sign-off relates to;

- Late project delivery: The use of MoSCoW prioritisation and Timeboxes give the mechanism for keeping the project on track and obtaining very early warning if on time delivery is threatened.

Risks to Atern Projects

- Low / patchy business roles

- Fully-detailed specification

- 100% solution expected

- Swapping team resources in and out

© TCC   DSATP/5/ 12

Risks to the success of a DSDM Atern project

- Low or patchy availability of business roles: DSDM Atern relies heavily on having the right level of involvement from the right business people throughout the project. Lack of availability of these resources may delay the project; lack of the right resources will compromise the project's products;

- Having a fully detailed specification at the outset: Where this is the case, the flexibility of DSDM Atern is removed – the ability to embrace change or to commit to a fixed time and cost are compromised;

- Expecting a 100% solution to be delivered within a specified time and budget: The control parameters of DSDM Atern are time, cost and functionality. The fourth dimension is quality. If 100% of the functionality is insisted upon within a fixed time and cost, there is a risk that quality will be compromised, which is an unacceptable situation in a DSDM Atern project;

- Swapping resources in and out of the DSDM Atern team: In a small DSDM Atern team, and with short Timeboxes, much information can be held informally between team members, if the team is stable. This speeds up progress and means that less documentation during the project is needed. However, if team members are constantly swapped in and out, this will increase the amount of documentation necessary for team communication, and also result in inconsistency of ideas and an additional learning curve for each new resource brought in. This, in turn, will threaten the meeting of Timebox deadlines and the quality of the end-product.

DSDM Atern-related project risks are assessed initially by completion of the Project Approach Questionnaire (PAQ), which is built from the DSDM Atern eight principles, the ISFs and other key factors. The PAQ can be used to negotiate a favourable start to the project. Matters that are not resolved favourably become risks to the project.

3.3   Configuration Management

Configuration Management is:

*'the process of identifying and defining the configuration items of a system, controlling the **release** and **change** of those items throughout the lifecycle, recording and reporting **status** of configuration items and change requests and **verifying completeness** and correctness of configuration items'*

ANSI/IEEE 729-1983.

A configuration item (CI) is a product of the project which needs to be recorded and protected from unauthorised change.

Configuration Management is about knowing what has been produced so far in a project (the CIs); knowing what state these items are in (finished, approved, work-in-progress); and where they are stored. It is also about protecting them from being damaged, destroyed or lost.

If our project is to build a house, we need to protect the incomplete building from vandalism or accidental damage; we need to know when the plumbing is finished and approved, in order that we do not start the plastering job too soon! We need to know when the house is finished, safe and ready for use.

In a software project, where the evolving product is not easily visible, we need to keep careful control of what has been built but not tested; tested but not released etc.

Formal Configuration Management (CM) of a project's assets is essential for all but the very smallest and simplest of projects. For DSDM Atern projects it is vital that Configuration Management fully supports the principles, practices and team behaviours that are required to make the approach as a whole successful.

The eight principles of Atern encapsulate the value of good Configuration Management. Configuration Management must be implemented in a way which does not contradict or compromise these principles.

Change control is intrinsically bound up with Configuration Management. Change control is the set of formal procedures that enable changes to be made to configuration items and record these changes. This must be applied so that it allows sufficient control to be kept. However, change control must not prevent change, which DSDM Atern embraces as an essential part of delivering the right product for the business.

In DSDM Atern, products are evolved through iterative development and prototyping, and are continually being improved upon. The integration of the completed product is also subject to Configuration Management.

Configuration Management is especially important in a DSDM Atern project because:

- DSDM Atern is dynamic and embraces change;

- Iterative development implies that a significant amount of change will intentionally take place, and this must be managed;

- It must be possible to back-track to a previous version of a product because of the way in which we develop products, discovering as we go;

- It must be clear which versions of products are current versions and which are older versions.

The Configuration Management process has to be ongoing throughout the project and will continue once the product becomes operational. If the product were a car, it is still necessary to know what items were used to assemble it (the 'bill of materials'), for servicing purposes.

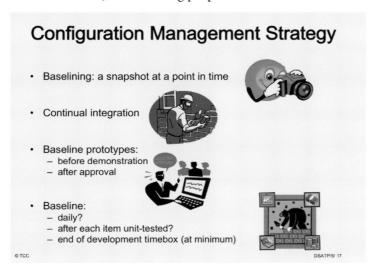

Configuration Management (CM) standards and procedures should be in place before the project commences, as there is no time to define these once the project is underway. It is imperative that the Solution Development Team members understand these procedures and the level at which Configuration Management occurs. Developers should be allowed to decide when a product they are working on is ready to become a Configuration Item, but it should be clear at what point this should be. If procedures are unclear, there is a danger that too much or too little baselining (i.e. committing of items into the CM system) will take place. Therefore, the CM approach needs a champion within the project who holds the responsibility for administering it and resolving any differences of opinion, etc., regarding its use. The CM Champion is often the Technical Co-ordinator. If the person undertaking that role is divorced from the rest of the Solution Development Team, then a team member should be the nominated CM champion within that team, so that change is under the control of the team, and external pressures do not slow it down or stifle it.

One benefit of good CM is that it will allow impact analysis of any future change.

Configuration Management strategy

A Configuration Management strategy must be decided as part of the Development Approach element of the Solution Foundations. It should be visible to all Solution Developers. At the very least, the strategy should cover the frequency at which changes will be baselined. Examples include:

- Baselining as part of Continual Integration of a solution;

- Baselining every prototype before demonstration;

- Baselining every prototype after an approval decision;

- Baselining daily, which enables flexibility but can be very onerous;

- Baselining software items once they have been unit-tested;

- Baselining at the end of a Development Timebox. This is the absolute minimum and should only be used if Timeboxes are short.

Configuration Items

A major question to be answered is what to select as Configuration Items, i.e. what has to be controlled in order to keep control of the project's emerging assets. The determination of which of the products of development become Configuration Items will be a balance between what is worth doing, achieving maximum flexibility in development whilst protecting the products which are being built.

Configuration Management is an important aspect of DSDM Atern projects, unless the project is very small and simple. CM enables the team to keep control of the solution as it evolves, to avoid duplication or conflict of effort, and to ensure that, at all times, reverting to the last agreed safe point (or baseline) is always possible.

3.4 Quality

In DSDM Atern, quality is about delivering a solution that is 'fit for purpose', i.e. delivering a working solution to meet the agreed acceptance criteria. The quality acceptance standard will vary from project to project, but once agreed and set (by the end of Foundations), it becomes the level that this project must achieve in order to be accepted and deemed fit for purpose. This decision, once made, fixes the quality level, in the same way that DSDM Atern fixes time and cost. Delivering a lower quality solution than agreed, just to meet the deadline or budget is not an option.

Aspects of quality

There are three aspects to quality which are directed toward the development of a right-quality product:

• Quality control;

• Quality assurance;

• Quality management (and a QM system).

Quality Control (QC) is the testing of a product and rejection of faulty products. Quality control may be achieved by inspection and review of products; dynamic testing of products; use of static analysis tools.

In DSDM Atern the bulk of quality control is performed by the Solution Development Team roles, which include a Solution Tester role. The Solution Developer has responsibility for ensuring that their work is tested for functionality. The Business Ambassador Role has responsibility for business acceptance of the project's products. A wider group of stakeholders may be involved in final acceptance of a product.

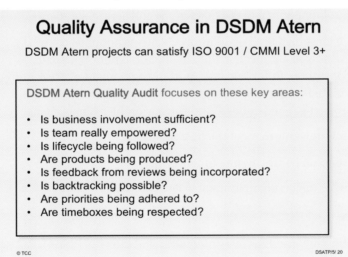

Quality Assurance (QA) is the definition of what products are intended to be produced, along with their acceptance criteria.

Quality Management (QM) is the planned use of the feedback from QC and QA activities to improve the process and standards for achieving the right quality of product.

The ISO9000 view of quality involves achieving customer satisfaction and meeting product requirement. This fits naturally with a DSDM Atern approach. The DSDM Atern techniques, both individually and in combination, help to ensure that the actual solution fits closely with what the business needs and expects. DSDM Atern has been recognised as an appropriate approach for ISO 9001 accreditation and is commonly used in organisations who wish to be Agile whilst achieving CMMI levels 3 and above.

The ISO standard on quality management can be interpreted as:

- Say what you are going to do;

- Do it;

- Then demonstrate that you have done it.

Within a DSDM Atern project, this process is adhered to:

- High level requirements are defined alongside their acceptance criteria;

- Within a development Timebox, more detailed definition of requirements evolves, along with more detailed acceptance criteria;

- During the development Timebox, the evolving solution is tested, against these acceptance criteria.

Distinct areas of quality

Quality in DSDM Atern typically focuses on two distinct areas:

- *Solution Quality:* This is an assessment of whether the solution delivers customer satisfaction; addresses the business needs; and has achieved the standards set for it;

- *Process Quality (Quality Management):* This measures whether the project follows the accepted best practices, set at organisational level. These may range from informal guidelines through to fully defined and audited ISO or CMMI processes and procedures.

DSDM Atern addresses both aspects of quality. Its practices and techniques naturally lead to a solution that meets expectations and agreed standards.

Solution Quality: If an agreed level of Solution Quality is not objectively defined and agreed early in a project, it will be difficult, if not impossible, to agree later what constitutes 'fit for purpose'. Without agreement of the required Solution Quality, shared by the whole project team, it becomes difficult to identify when a product is 'good enough' and various problems may ensue:

- The delivered solution fails to meet the business need;

- The delivered solution has the wrong functionality;

- The delivered solution has an unacceptable level of flaws;

- Ongoing support becomes expensive, risky and time-consuming;

- The delivered solution is unnecessarily complex and puts the project timescales at risk.

Process Quality: For an Agile approach, all activities should add benefit to the end results. Quality-related activities are sometimes perceived as bureaucratic and adding no value. An organisation's approach to quality must be flexible enough to meet the needs of an Agile project. A DSDM Atern project should be able to demonstrate control but the 'level of ceremony' demanded by the Process Quality management system should be appropriate for an Agile approach.

Maintainability and quality

Although maintenance typically happens once the project moves into support, it has to be considered from the very beginning of the project. Solutions with poor maintainability result in a higher Total Cost of Ownership (TCO) as they:

- Take more resources to maintain;
- Take longer to change and cost more to change;
- Are more likely to introduce further errors with change;
- Will be unreliable;
- May slow the development of future increments;
- Are a risk to the business.

Maintainability objectives

In a DSDM Atern project, there are three possible levels of maintainability:

- *Level 1 – maintainability is a required attribute of the initial delivered solution:* The requirement is for a supportable solution from the first increment. The criterion for deployment is to provide the required functionality in a robust way and to ensure the components for each increment can be fully supported before the solution is accepted and released to the business.

- *Level 2 – deliver first, re-engineer later:* The business priority is to elicit and implement the required functionality quickly. However because the solution needs a long life and must be maintainable in the longer term, the business is prepared to pay for subsequent (behind the scenes) re-engineering after implementation. This means a greater development cost than building for maintainability first time, but gives a quicker initial delivery. It may also produce a lower lifetime TCO. This option is often chosen when time to market is critical. For this option, it is important to ensure sizing and funding has been agreed for the later re-engineering work. Otherwise, it may never happen.

- *Level 3 – short-term, tactical solution:* This is used when early delivery is the target and maintainability is not considered to be important (the solution will be replaced or rewritten before maintenance costs become a problem – typically this is a one-off or temporary solution). It is particularly important that any decision to build a tactical solution is documented and the expected life is agreed, as there is a tendency for such solutions to become long-term corporate business solutions and therefore potentially a risk and expense to the organisation.

A final decision must be made during Foundations as to which of these three levels applies.

As for all key non-functional requirements, once the decision on maintainability has been made, the risks of the chosen approach must be defined and managed.

The maintainability decision, taken at the start of the project, should be reaffirmed at all major milestones of the development.

Quality planning and reviews

Quality planning should be an integral part of the DSDM Atern project's planning activities. Projects also need to be reviewed from time to time:

- In order to determine their compliance with the organisation's procedures, practices and standards;

- To assess the health of a project, based on whether it is following recommended best practice. This can be used to identify 'at risk' projects and allows measures to get them back on track, to put them on hold or to stop them. This may be a formal Gateway Review, with a Go / No-go decision.

Some key questions to consider when reviewing (auditing) a DSDM Atern project include:

- Is there sufficient business involvement to support the approach?

- Is the team empowered?

- Is the lifecycle being followed?

- Are the products being produced?

- Are comments from reviews being incorporated?

- Is backtracking possible?

- Are priorities being adhered to?

- Are Timeboxes being respected?

3.5 Testing in DSDM Atern

Testing is integrated throughout the DSDM Atern lifecycle. Testing in DSDM Atern is based on the following eight concepts:

- Fail Fast;

- Collaborative;

- Repeatable;

- End-to-End;

- Independent;

- Prioritised;

- Test-driven Development;

- Risk-based.

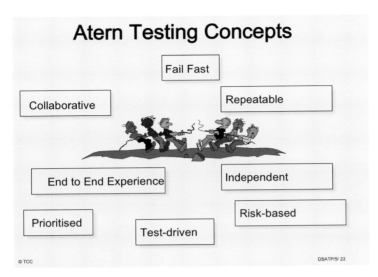

Atern Testing Concepts

Fail Fast

Collaborative

Repeatable

End to End Experience

Independent

Prioritised

Test-driven

Risk-based

© TCC

DSATP/5/ 23

Fail Fast

It is well-established that the earlier a defect is found, the less it costs to fix. Therefore we should test early and continuously throughout the lifecycle.

Collaborative

All of the Solution Development Team have responsibilities related to testing. Their collaboration is essential during the test-fix-retest cycle.

Repeatable

Because of the iterative nature of DSDM Atern development, it is likely that the same test will need to be run many times, including regression testing to enable the frequent incremental deliveries. The Solution Development Team must plan to ensure efficiency of these test re-runs.

End-to-End

Testing the end-to-end experience includes usability, performance and process testing, and is linked to the iterative development perspectives: functional; usability; non-functional. The capability/technique prototype may be used to test the end-to-end experience with an architectural spike.

Independent

A product should always be tested by someone other than its producer. The DSDM Atern roles ensure that the Solution Development Team always has an independent perspective which may be applied.

Prioritised

It is not possible to exhaustively test every aspect of a complex product, in every scenario of its use. The cost effective way to test, therefore, is to prioritise the tests which are done. This may be to undertake:

- Error-centric testing (test where errors are likely to be found, around boundaries for example);

- Benefit-directed testing (testing the parts of the system likely to give greatest benefit, or to contain greatest risk. MoSCoW prioritisation can be used effectively here).

Test-driven Development

An effective Agile approach is to write tests (or acceptance criteria) before development of the product. This way, the product can be defined before any effort is expended on building the wrong thing.

Risk-based

Product risk can be assessed by evaluating the probability of failure and the impact if failure occurs. By using this approach to calculate the higher-risk areas of a solution, tests can be focused on areas where failure would be most costly.

3.6 Testing products and the testing approach

DSDM Atern makes a clear distinction between Technical and Business testing: These aspects of testing answer the questions:

- Is the product being built right (Technical testing)?

- Is the right product being built (Business testing)?

The DSDM Atern roles have clearly defined responsibilities related to testing. The products associated with testing in Atern fall into two categories:

- Business Domain products: the Business Testing Strategy and the Business Testing Pack;

- Solution Domain products: the System Testing Strategy and the System Testing Pack.

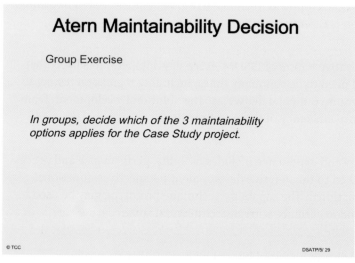

Atern Maintainability Decision

Group Exercise

In groups, decide which of the 3 maintainability options applies for the Case Study project.

© TCC   DSATP/5/ 29

These products map to the Business and Technical testing responsibilities.

As far as the testing approach is concerned, a key feature is to ensure that the purpose of testing is clearly defined before the test. At some points (e.g. an initial iteration of investigation) the testing may be to ensure that the expected information has been gleaned, rather than that anything is actually working and producing results. At the final iteration (consolidation) within an Engineering development Timebox, it is likely that a fully-working product is the expected result. There are different perspectives of iterative development including usability, business, and performance/capacity impact on the expected results of testing, and it is essential that the team are aware of just what perspective is being tested.

3.7 Metrics

Metrics are a useful tool for the Project Manager and the team. Measurement of effort against the progress achieved enables a project to improve its estimating, and there is an immediate payback from this in a Timeboxed environment, where planning is incremental.

Metrics in Atern

- Immediate payback in an iterative environment

- Why measure?

- Keep it simple, make it easy

- What are we measuring?

- Compare measures (need > 1!)

- Measures drive behaviour

© TCC   DSATP/5/ 26

A few useful guidelines for collecting metrics are:

- Keep it simple, make metrics easy to collect;

- Be clear about what is being measured, and look at outcomes, not outputs;

- Compare measures – one figure alone rarely tells enough of a story. Look at using metrics over time and collecting comparative figures;

- Finally, remember that measures drive behaviour. If speed of arrival at an accident is the only measure of success for the ambulance crew, they do not need all of that heavy equipment on the ambulance slowing them down!

4. Conclusion

Managing DSDM Atern projects relies on having a Project Manager who focuses on motivating and supporting their empowered teams, rather than micro-managing at a task level. The Atern Project Manager helps keep the team on track, by ensuring Atern best practice is being followed. Progress is demonstrated and measured in terms of delivery of a working product.

Project Management Considerations

1. **What approach should the Project Manager in a DSDM Atern project take to managing the team?**

   A} A rigid, inflexible approach

   B} A completely 'hands-off' approach

   C} A collaborative, supportive approach

   D} A dictatorial approach

2. **Traditional project approaches focus on a fixed specification, and time and resource may vary. DSDM Atern expects the specification to be:**

   A} Fixed, but quality may vary

   B} Flexible, with a fixed time and budget

   C} Fixed, with a fixed time and cost

   D} Flexible, but time and cost may also vary

3. **The DSDM Atern Project Manager focuses on:**

   A} Motivating and supporting the empowered teams

   B} Micro-managing the teams at a task level

   C} Recording 'actuals' and writing the team's documentation

   D} Watching the team for career appraisal purposes

4. **At the Daily Stand-up, each team member states:**

   A} Their life history

   B} Any problems or issues they have encountered which are threatening the plan

   C} The detailed design of areas of the solution they are working on

   D} Which aspects of the work they are enjoying the most

5. **The Daily Stand-up is a meeting which:**

   A} Is secret, attended by the Solution Development Team only

   B} May be attended by any appropriate DSDM Atern project personnel

   C} Is always a full meeting of all project stakeholders

   D} Only for the technical roles in the team

Answers can be found on page 222

Dynamic Systems Development
Method

Project Management Considerations

Session Objectives

- DSDM Atern Project Management

- Major Planning Issues:
  - Control
  - Risk
  - Configuration Management
  - Quality
  - Testing
  - Metrics
  - Maintainability

Traditional v. Atern Project Management

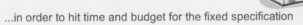

Traditional:
- Strict adherence to specification
- Control of resource

...in order to hit time and budget for the fixed specification

Atern:
- Evolutionary change to specification
- Collaborative, 'no-blame' user/developer relationship
- Timeboxing

...to deliver a valuable element of the solution on time

© TCC   DSATP/5/ 3

Atern Project Managers must:

- Understand the business and technical issues

- Facilitate the team
  (arbitrate <u>not</u> dictate)

- Avoid 'burnout' of team members
  (allow sustainable pace)

© TCC   DSATP/5/ 4

Communication

- An environment conducive to good communication

- Team members who are good communicators

- Co-located teams, where possible

- Daily "Stand-ups"

- Facilitated workshops & retrospectives

- Modelling and prototyping

Major Planning Issues

- Control and plans

- Risk Management

- Configuration Management

- Quality & Testing

- Metrics

- Maintainability

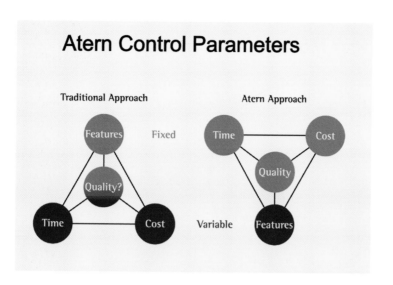

Atern Control Parameters

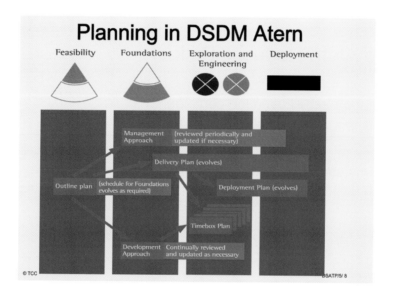

Planning in DSDM Atern

What is Risk?

A project risk is something that may happen …

If it does, it will have a detrimental effect!

A Typical Risk Management Process

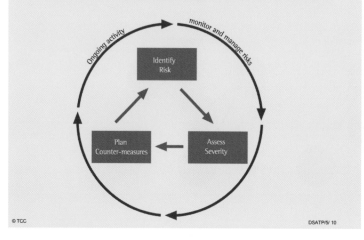

Where Atern Reduces Risk

- Traditional approaches use time contingency
- Agile NDUF, traditional BDUF

- Requirements unknowable up-front
- Requirements change

- Sign off

Risks to Atern Projects

- Low / patchy business roles

- Fully-detailed specification

- 100% solution expected

- Swapping team resources in and out

Atern Risk Exercise

Group Exercise

- What are 3 key **ATERN** risks to the Case Study project?

- How would you mitigate these?

What is Configuration Management?

© TCC
DSATP/5/ 14

Configuration Management

Configuration Management is the process of:

- **Identifying and defining** configuration items (CIs) of a system

- **Controlling release and change** of CIs throughout the lifecycle

- **Recording and reporting status** of CIs and change requests

- **Verifying completeness and correctness** of CIs

ANSI/IEEE 729

Change Control : the set of formal procedures which record and enable changes to configuration items.

© TCC
DSATP/5/ 15

Configuration Management

Why is CM necessary?

- Iteration implies change, which must be managed
- Changes must be reversible - version control
- Solution developers need to be confident of right version

CM Champion

- Tech. Co-ordinator?
- Within team

Tool Support?

Configuration Management Strategy

- Baselining: a snapshot at a point in time

- Continual integration

- Baseline prototypes:
  - before demonstration
  - after approval

- Baseline:
  - daily?
  - after each item unit-tested?
  - end of development timebox (at minimum)

Atern Configuration Management Exercise

Group Exercise

- Who would **you** put in charge of CM in the Case Study?

- What would you expect their **biggest challenge** to CM to be?

Prepare 2 or 3 points to discuss with the other groups

What is Quality?
"Fitness for Purpose"

Quality Control (testing and rejection of faulty products)	**Quality Assurance** (definition of products and quality criteria)

 Solution Quality

 Process Quality

Quality Management and a QM system
(the feedback from QC & QA to improve
the process using a system of tools, techniques
and standards etc)

© TCC   DSATP/5/ 19

Quality Assurance in DSDM Atern

DSDM Atern projects can satisfy ISO 9001 / CMMI Level 3+

DSDM Atern Quality Audit focuses on these key areas:

- Is business involvement sufficient?
- Is team really empowered?
- Is lifecycle being followed?
- Are products being produced?
- Is feedback from reviews being incorporated?
- Is backtracking possible?
- Are priorities being adhered to?
- Are timeboxes being respected?

Quality Management

" ...say what you are going to do,

do it,

demonstrate that you have done it... "

© TCC   DSATP/5/ 21

Quality Related Activities

- **Inspection & review** against product descriptions

- **Dynamic testing**

- **Static testing**

- **Review/demonstration** of key prototypes

Atern Testing Concepts

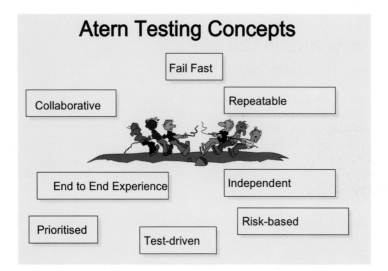

Fail Fast

Collaborative

Repeatable

End to End Experience

Independent

Prioritised

Test-driven

Risk-based

Atern "Key Techniques" in Testing

Group Exercise

- Modelling

- MoSCoW Prioritisation

- Facilitated Workshops

*In groups, decide how the above techniques
could help in testing in an Atern project*

Atern 5 Key Techniques

- MoSCoW Prioritisation

- Modelling

- Facilitated Workshops

- Iterative Development

- Timeboxing

© TCC   DSATP/5/ 25

Metrics in Atern

- Immediate payback in an iterative environment

- Why measure?

- Keep it simple, make it easy

- What are we measuring?

- Compare measures (need > 1!)

- Measures drive behaviour

Atern Metrics

Group Exercise

*In groups, think of one simple (but imaginative!) metric
which would measure the success of the Case Study project*

Maintainability v Cost

Senior Management **decision at outset:**

 Maintainability a requirement for the new system

OR

 Maintainability is not a problem: short system life, replaced before maintenance an issue

OR

 Maintainability secondary to rapid delivery. The business will accept cost of re-engineering

DSATP/5/ 28

Atern Maintainability Decision

Group Exercise

In groups, decide which of the 3 maintainability options applies for the Case Study project.

Session Summary

- DSDM Atern Project Management

- Major Planning Issues
  - Control
  - Configuration Management
  - Risk
  - Quality
  - Testing
  - Metrics
  - Maintainability

Dynamic Systems Development Method

Project Management Considerations

6. Facilitated Workshops

1. Introduction

Workshops are meetings of a particular format, held to achieve a particular purpose quickly and effectively. They involve the appropriate stakeholders to achieve the workshop objective (business representatives, Solution Development personnel etc.) which may be, for example to:

- Obtain decisions;
- Extract information;
- Design aspects of a system;
- Create a plan;
- Obtain agreement;
- Establish commitment;
- Secure approval.

A Facilitated Workshop is often the best technique for eliciting a key business or technical decision from a group of people, either within one organisation, or in some cases including customers and suppliers.

2. Facilitated Workshops in DSDM Atern

Facilitated Workshops have been used in business and in business systems development in particular, for many years. Initially they were used for Joint Requirements Planning (JRP workshops) and Joint Application Design (JAD workshops). Since then, their value has been recognised in other areas. They are a core technique in DSDM Atern for achieving consensus, building plans and capturing requirements, and as a way of making high quality, team-based decisions in short timescales.

This section examines how the approach maps directly onto DSDM Atern and where in DSDM Atern they can be used. It seeks to show the potential uses of Facilitated Workshops in a DSDM Atern project. It is up to the project members themselves to decide whether a workshop is necessary, or whether another technique, such as interviewing or research is more applicable.

Facilitated Workshops are a useful tool for effecting cultural change in an organisation because they promote buy-in from and empowerment of participants. When used effectively, they can set a positive tone for the whole project.

3. What are Facilitated Workshops?

3.1 Definition

A Facilitated Workshop is a structured approach to enable a group of people to work towards a predefined objective in a short timeframe, supported by an impartial Facilitator.

3.2 Benefits

Using Facilitated Workshops brings both direct and indirect benefits to a project:

- Rapid, quality decision-making: If the appropriate group of stakeholders are present at the same time, there is typically great confidence in the result. The group is focused on the objectives to be achieved in the session so that the information gathering and review cycle is performed at a greater speed. Also, misunderstandings and disagreements can be worked out at the time. Any concerns should have been raised and resolved or noted by the end of the workshop;

- Greater user buy-in by all stakeholders: Workshops, run effectively, lead to participants feeling more involved in the project and the decisions being made. They build and maintain enthusiasm;

- Building team spirit: A workshop is a controlled way of building rapport as well as delivering results. It can promote understanding and co-operation between departments, which is particularly important when a project involves many groups;

- Process redesign by the user community: If working practices are reviewed as a result of a workshop, participants can gain a greater understanding of the inputs and implications of their work. This can lead to improved efficiencies that are led by the participants themselves, giving greater buy-in and commitment and, therefore, a greater chance of successful deployment;

- Clarification of requirements and issues: Business users can be led through their objectives and processes by the Facilitator, to define what they may require. In the facilitated environment, participants can explore and model ideas. This is made possible through a combination of structured discussion and the presence of the appropriate, knowledgeable participants.

Workshop Benefits

- Rapid, high quality decision-making

- Greater buy-in

- Building team spirit

- Building consensus

- Clarification of issues

© TCC   DSATP/6/7

4. Aligning Workshops to the DSDM Atern Framework and Workshop Roles to DSDM Atern Roles

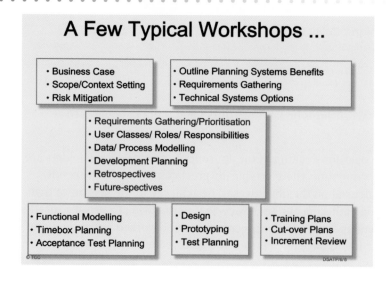

A Few Typical Workshops …

- Business Case
- Scope/Context Setting
- Risk Mitigation

- Outline Planning Systems Benefits
- Requirements Gathering
- Technical Systems Options

- Requirements Gathering/Prioritisation
- User Classes/ Roles/ Responsibilities
- Data/ Process Modelling
- Development Planning
- Retrospectives
- Future-spectives

- Functional Modelling
- Timebox Planning
- Acceptance Test Planning

- Design
- Prototyping
- Test Planning

- Training Plans
- Cut-over Plans
- Increment Review

© TCC   DSATP/6/8

This section gives some guidance on which DSDM Atern roles would fill the roles of a workshop. The workshop roles are:

- Workshop Owner;
- Facilitator;
- Participant;
- Observer;
- Co-Facilitator;
- Scribe.

4.1 Workshop Owner

This is the owner of the problem that the workshop is set to solve. It is up to them to work with the Facilitator to set the objectives and deliverables of the workshop, although these should also be understood clearly and agreed by the participants.

The owner of a Feasibility Assessment workshop could be the Business Sponsor, whereas the owner of a Timebox planning session could be the Project Manager, Team Leader or even the Business Ambassador.

4.2 Facilitator

The Facilitator should be impartial, with no stake in the outcome of the workshop, and ideally come from outside the project. The role of the Facilitator is to manage the structure and dynamics of the workshop. The Facilitator maps directly onto the DSDM Atern role of Workshop Facilitator.

4.3 Participant

Participants are the individuals who are knowledgeable in the areas under consideration within the workshop and empowered to represent the views of other project stakeholders (e.g. the business and software development communities).

A participant could be one of many roles within the project. They could be a business user, a customer, a supplier, a business analyst, a data modeller, a systems architect, a member of the financial staff, an auditor, or indeed any of the DSDM Atern project level roles, Solution Development Team or specialist roles.

4.4 Observer

Observer is not a required role of a Facilitated Workshop. However, from time to time, individuals are present at a workshop who have no participative role. These are classed as observers. The observer is not meant to contribute towards the output of the workshop. If they need to take part at all, they should be classed clearly as a participant and be involved fully in the workshop proceedings. Examples of an observer include: someone auditing the workshop process or the Facilitator's ability; a trainee Facilitator who would want to observe the group dynamics without being part of the group; a manager, wishing to see progress of the project first-hand; a trainee or someone new to the project, wishing to get 'up to speed'. Observers could also be development or support staff gathering useful background information, but in these cases it should be checked whether they are in fact participants and should be actively contributing to the session.

4.5 Co-Facilitator

A Co-Facilitator works alongside the Facilitator capturing output from the workshop on flipcharts and whiteboards. They also provide a second view on the performance of the participants and give feedback to the Facilitator.

4.6 Scribe

The Scribe, or Co-Facilitator, records what is happening within the workshop. The role could be held by someone involved in the project: a business analyst, solution developer or user, so long as the individual has the required understanding of the issues in order to know what to record. There is a downside to this: the Scribe's participation in the workshop will be limited by the role. Therefore, the choice of a Scribe should be considered carefully. There may sometimes be a need for more than one Scribe in a workshop. For example, one Scribe may record issues and actions on paper or flip charts, whilst another uses a software tool to directly model or record the product of the workshop.

5. Applying the DSDM Atern Principles Within a Facilitated Workshop

A Facilitated Workshop is like a DSDM Atern project in miniature: defined deliverables; tight Timebox; empowered participants. Early workshops can help to build the firm foundation which continues throughout the project. The list below shows how some of the DSDM Atern principles apply in Facilitated Workshops:

- Collaborate: Workshops provide an ideal format for the business to be directly involved in planning, designing and implementing a solution. Workshop participants need to be empowered and have the right level of knowledge and authority within the scope of the workshop, so that decisions can be made without delay. The Facilitator is responsible for creating the climate of co-operation within the workshop and enforcing any ground rules for the group to behave effectively. This is only possible with the co-operation and commitment of all stakeholders. It is an effective way of achieving either compromise or consensus.

- Build incrementally from firm foundations: It is good practice to structure a workshop so that there are intermediate deliverables. It helps to order participants' thinking as they progress in logical steps. This enables them to work towards an ultimate goal and gives them a growing sense of achievement as the workshop progresses. The Facilitator checks that fitness for purpose is achieved by keeping participants focused on delivery against an agreed set of objectives. They ensure all are involved in decision-making.

- Develop iteratively: One of the strengths of workshops is the synergy achieved by the group. Objectives must be set during the preparation for a workshop. As the workshop progresses, information is gathered, analysed and interpreted so that discussion can be effective and a decision reached as a result of an increased understanding of the issues involved. Ideas do not have to be fully developed from the outset but can grow during discussion. In effect, they are being prototyped. It is an ideal setting to try out ideas with all stakeholders and it is up to the Facilitator to provide a safe environment in which this may happen. Information and decisions should be recorded as necessary, by either one or both of the Facilitator and Scribe, so that ideas can be backtracked where necessary. Often what happens in practice is that an idea or decision is redeveloped.

- Never compromise quality: Because all appropriate stakeholders are present, this provides the quality control approach of testing ideas and deliverables as they are produced. Participants have the opportunity to challenge or agree.

6. Workshops Within the DSDM Atern Lifecycle

Table 6.1 shows some of the commonly-used workshop types. It is not intended to be an exhaustive or definitive list but may be helpful in deciding where workshops are appropriate in a project.

The list gives suggestions for the types of workshop that could be run during a project. Some of them could be combined and become sessions within a longer workshop. Depending on the size and complexity of the problems being addressed, it may not always be necessary to set up a Facilitated Workshop session; workshop techniques could still be used in an informal interactive session. The duration of workshops varies, depending upon the product to be produced and the necessary number of participants.

DSDM Atern Lifecycle Phase	Typical Workshop Types
Feasibility	Problem definition
	Solution options evaluation
	Context setting
	Estimating
	Business case building
	Risk analysis
	Project approach questionnaire
	Outline planning
	Risk mitigation planning
	Prototype design
	Prototype review
Foundations	User classes definition
	Requirements gathering
	Prioritisation
	Process modelling
	Data modelling
	Solution architecture definition
	Test strategy definition
	Solution prototyping
	Timeboxing strategy definition
	Delivery planning
	Operational readiness criteria
	Roles and responsibilities definition
	Risk mitigation planning

Exploration	Timebox planning
	Problem resolution
	Functional modelling
	Process modelling
	Data modelling
	Scenario modelling
	Process and roles cross matching
	Prototype design
	Prototype review
	Risk mitigation planning
	Deployment planning
	Data conversion requirements
	Training needs analysis
	Training plans
	Timebox retrospectives
Engineering	Timebox planning
	Risk mitigation planning
	Problem resolution
	Prototype design
	Design prototype review
	Test planning
	Timebox retrospectives
	Test reviews
Deployment	User documentation requirements
	Support documentation requirements
	Training needs analysis
	Training plans
	Cutover plans
	Contingency planning
	Support level definition
	Problem resolution
	Increment review
Post-Project	Post implementation review
	Benefits realisation assessment

Table 6.1 Commonly-used workshop types

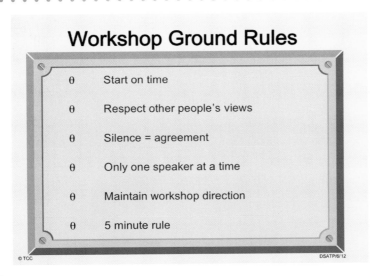

Workshop Ground Rules

- θ   Start on time
- θ   Respect other people's views
- θ   Silence = agreement
- θ   Only one speaker at a time
- θ   Maintain workshop direction
- θ   5 minute rule

© TCC   DSATP/6/12

7.1 The Facilitator

A Workshop should be run by a skilled Facilitator. The Facilitator should be impartial to the issues under discussion with no stake in the outcome of the workshop. Facilitation is a highly skilled role requiring sensitivity, diplomacy, quick thinking and highly developed communication skills. The role is instrumental in ensuring a workshop is successful. The Facilitator will manage the workshop process so that all participants have an equal opportunity to contribute and are able to work as a team. The Facilitator ensures that there is sufficient documentation of the results and decisions from the workshop, often working with a Scribe to provide a 'group memory' of the event.

7.2 Objectives

Objectives should be set for the workshop and checked for their alignment with the scope of the whole project. They should be set by the owner and agreed by participants, but the Facilitator should check for measurability and any priority.

7.3 Scope

Along with the objectives, the scope of the workshop should be defined. This could be described in terms of business functions, organisational lines or other defining limits.

7.4 Participants

Without the right people present for the workshop, a solution of the right quality cannot be reached. The owner should suggest who the participants should be, but this should be reviewed by the participants themselves and checked for 'reasonableness' by the Facilitator. Participants need to be committed to the success of the workshop, empowered and appropriately prepared.

7.5 Intermediate deliverables

If the workshop is structured so that the route to the final deliverable is clear, it will make it easier to review progress during the workshop.

7.6 Workshop reports

Workshop outputs should be produced as soon as possible after the workshop. An efficient Scribe may be able to provide outputs for participants to take away from the workshop. In any event, results of the workshop should be with participants no more than 48 hours after the event.

8. Facilitated Workshop Activities

The activities associated with a Facilitated Workshop are:

- Plan the workshop;

- Prepare for the workshop;

- The workshop session:

  - Run the workshop;

  - Review the workshop;

- Document the workshop;

- Follow-up.

Facilitated Workshop Success Factors

- Good Facilitator, trained for the job
- Flexibility of format but NOT objectives
- Preparation
- Education (preparation session before Workshop)

  - Earlier results built in
  - User solution facilitated, <u>not forced</u>
  - Review of good/bad points
  - Feedback of results to participants

- Suitability of Workshops to organisational culture?

© TCC   DSATP/6/14

8.1 Plan the workshop

The workshop owner defines the objectives of the workshop and identifies the necessary participants. It may sometimes be necessary to define several workshops to achieve the objectives. The size of the workshop should ideally be in the range of six to twelve people (more can be accommodated if necessary, but additional planning and structuring is required).

8.2 Prepare for the workshop

In preparation for the workshop, the Facilitator must circulate information to the participants so that they fully understand the objective of the workshop and the background to it. The workshop agenda detailing when, where and who will be attending, as well as the order of proceedings, should be sent out reasonably in advance of the event, together with any pre-workshop reading. In particular, individuals will be advised of what input to the workshop is needed so that they may prepare beforehand in order to make an effective contribution.

8.3 Run the workshop

The tight timescales of a DSDM Atern project mean that the workshop needs to maintain its focus. Some Facilitators operate on the principle of a five-minute rule where any disagreement that cannot be resolved in a period of five minutes is declared an 'open issue'. Such open issues are documented and deferred to a later session or referred to the Business Sponsor, if appropriate.

8.4 Review the workshop

The effectiveness of the workshop should be examined and any lessons learnt fed back into the operation of future workshops. In particular, did the workshop meet its objectives fully or only partially; did all participants contribute to the process; did it run to time?

8.5 Document the workshop

The Scribe produces and distributes a workshop report to the workshop owner and all participants. The workshop report documents:

- Decisions taken;

- Actions agreed and to whom they are assigned;

- Open issues;

- The product which was the objective of the workshop.

8.6 Follow-up

The workshop owner must be consulted to confirm satisfaction with the workshop's results. All actions marked for follow-up activity outside the workshop forum must be addressed not just documented!

9. Benefits of Facilitated Workshops

Facilitated Workshops are a quick way of eliciting information and provide a forum for the resolution of conflict and differences of opinion. They give a sense of involvement to participants and gain ownership for the developing product. However, it is essential that the key decision-makers are involved and that the workshops are empowered to make decisions about the direction of the developing system, otherwise progress will be hampered. By bringing people together from a number of business areas in a Facilitated Workshop, a broader perspective of the project is created. Understanding is therefore improved and better decisions can be made for the business. Clear workshop ground rules and a clear decision-making framework are needed to ensure workshop effectiveness.

10. Conclusion

Facilitated Workshops are a particularly effectively form of meeting, held to achieve a particular purpose quickly. They involve the appropriate participants to meet the workshop objectives.

For success, a Facilitated Workshop should have:

- A skilled, trained Facilitator;

- Flexibility in the format of the workshop, but clearly defined objectives;

- Thorough preparation before the workshop by all parties;

- A mechanism for ensuring that previous workshop results are built in;

- A solution or agreement that is not forced. If the workshop participants cannot agree on a point (perhaps due to lack of information) within the workshop, the Facilitator should seek a solution from the group to remedy the shortfall;

- A review at the end of each workshop, documenting the plus and minus points of the workshop;

- A workshop report, which participants should receive, detailing decisions, actions and the product of the workshop, as soon as possible after the workshop;

- A format suited to the culture of the organisation. (Assess whether this collaborative method of working is acceptable to the organisation.)

Facilitated Workshops

1. **A workshop will:**

   A} Encourage collaborative working

   B} Allow people to see who is not working hard enough

   C} Extend the project timescales

   D} Only be effective if all members of the project team are present

2. **A trained Workshop Facilitator:**

   A} Creates an environment that allows full participation by everyone in the workshop

   B} Demonstrates control at all times

   C} Always chooses the workshop participants

   D} Keeps order by setting the ground rules

3. **DSDM Atern emphasises the value of human interaction through:**

   A} Strong control of meetings

   B} Facilitated Workshops, clearly defined roles and user involvement

   C} Stage-end meetings

   D} Well written textual documents

4. **Who sets the objectives for a workshop?**

   A} Workshop Owner

   B} Facilitator

   C} Workshop Scribe

   D} Project Manager

5. **A well-run Facilitated Workshop will deliver the following:**

   A} An outcome in half a day

   B} An outcome to satisfy the Business Sponsor

   C} A result which cannot be changed

   D} An outcome with a high degree of buy-in and ownership

Answers can be found on page 222

Dynamic Systems Development Method

Atern

Facilitated Workshops

Session Content

- What is a Facilitated Workshop?

- Workshop types

- Workshop roles

- Planning and dynamics

- Success factors

Atern 5 Key Techniques

- MoSCoW Prioritisation

- Modelling

- Facilitated Workshops

- Iterative Development

- Timeboxing

© TCC   DSATP/6/3

What is a Facilitated Workshop?

- A place where a specific job of work is done ... and a product produced.

  - A team-based information gathering and decision making technique

  - Interactive communication
  - Empowered personnel
  - Independent facilitator

What is a Facilitator?

- A helper and enabler
- A referee, not a player

One who contributes to

structure and *process (not content)*

So that groups can function effectively

and make high-quality decisions

© TCC

DSATP/6/5

Why Have Facilitated Workshops?

- 3 things they are good for
- 3 risks

Group Exercise

Workshop Benefits

- Rapid, high quality decision-making

- Greater buy-in

- Building team spirit

- Building consensus

- Clarification of issues

A Few Typical Workshops ...

- Business Case
- Scope/Context Setting
- Risk Mitigation

- Outline Planning Systems Benefits
- Requirements Gathering
- Technical Systems Options

- Requirements Gathering/Prioritisation
- User Classes/ Roles/ Responsibilities
- Data/ Process Modelling
- Development Planning
- Retrospectives
- Future-spectives

- Functional Modelling
- Timebox Planning
- Acceptance Test Planning

- Design
- Prototyping
- Test Planning

- Training Plans
- Cut-over Plans
- Increment Review

© TCC

DSATP/6/8

Workshop Roles

Workshop Owner

Observer(s)

PARTICIPANTS

Workshop Facilitator

Workshop Co-Facilitator

Workshop Scribe(s)

© TCC

DSATP/6/9

Planning Facilitated Workshops

What 5 aspects do we need to plan,
for a Facilitated Workshop?

Group Exercise

Workshop Planning

- Workshop definition (owner, product, participants)
- Prepare for Workshop (objective-driven agenda)

> - Run Workshop session
> - Review Workshop

- Final document - Workshop Report
- Review with Workshop Owner

Workshop Ground Rules

θ	Start on time
θ	Respect other people's views
θ	Silence = agreement
θ	Only one speaker at a time
θ	Maintain workshop direction
θ	5 minute rule

Is a Workshop the Best Way?

Facilitated Workshop Success Factors

- Good Facilitator, trained for the job
- Flexibility of format but NOT objectives
- Preparation
- Education (preparation session before Workshop)

  - Earlier results built in
  - User solution facilitated, <u>not forced</u>
  - Review of good/bad points
  - Feedback of results to participants

- Suitability of Workshops to organisational culture?

© TCC   DSATP/6/14

Session Summary

- What is a Facilitated Workshop?

- Workshop roles

- Workshop types

- Planning and dynamics

- Success factors

Dynamic Systems Development Method

Facilitated Workshops

Requirements Definition and Prioritisation

1. What is a Requirement?

At its simplest, a requirement is a service or function that a user wishes the solution provided by the project to perform, or a feature that the solution should exhibit.

For example, in a training company with its own training centre:

- The course manager has a requirement to schedule training courses;
- The training centre manager has a requirement to keep track of what training is running;
- The financial accountant has a requirement to maximise the amount of time that the training rooms are in use (thereby maximising revenue).

If the product of the project is a custom-built car, the requirements may be more feature-based:

- A means of propulsion;
- A maintainable steering capability;
- A comfortable place to sit.

It should be noticed that the following are actually solutions rather than requirements:

- An engine;
- A steering wheel;
- Bucket seats.

More flexibility can be retained if requirements are kept to 'What' rather than 'How' for as long as possible.

What is a Requirement?

In simple terms, a requirement is a:

- Feature
- Function
- Service
- Constraint

...that the solution needs to perform or exhibit

© TCC   DSATP/

2. Categories of Requirement

In broad terms, there are two categories of requirement: functional and non-functional.

Defining the Requirements

- Define a requirement along with its Acceptance Criteria as measurable targets at all levels.

- Give it a unique ID

- Keep details of:
  - Source
  - Owner
  - Business benefit
  - Priority
  - Other?

2.1 Functional requirements

Functional requirements answer the question, 'WHAT will the solution do?'

These will be expressed in terms of a business function or service, for example:

- Generate monthly reports on training room usage;

- Capture details of all scheduled courses.

Functional requirements are specified at a high level during Foundations and then decomposed further into more specific, detailed requirements during Exploration.

Functional Requirements

- Functional Requirement is "what", not "how"

- Make it SMART
  - Specific
  - Measurable
  - Achievable
  - Realistic
  - Timely

- Wording - Functional Requirement:
  - "We need the ability to …"
  - "As a … I need … in order to …"

- Not in conflict with, or overlapping, other requirements

© TCC   DSATP/7/6

2.2 Non-functional requirements

Non-functional requirements are those features of a requirement that tell us HOW WELL, or to what level the requirement is to be performed. This is in terms of any constraints, restrictions (e.g. security) or expectations (e.g. response times of less than two seconds). They define the level to which the solution should operate, rather than what it should do. Every functional requirement will normally be subject to one or more non-functional features, which form part of the acceptance criteria for the requirement and enable the analyst and user to agree whether or not the requirement has actually been met satisfactorily.

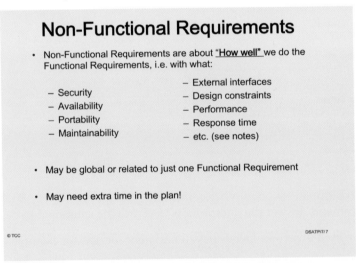

Non-functional requirements may be global and apply across the whole (or significant areas) of the solution or they may be specific to an individual functional requirement or a group of functional requirements.

Non-functional requirements can be considered under the following typical, main categories:

- *Performance requirements:* These specify numerical values for the measurable variables within the solution, such as response rates, capacity volumes and communication rates;

- *Interface requirements:* These specify the other products or areas that the solution must fit in with. For example, in an IT system, the hardware or software elements with which the new system, or system component, must interact or communicate;

- *Operational requirements:* These specify how the solution will run and communicate with its users. Operational requirements include all user interface and support requirements;

- *Resource requirements:* These specify the limits on physical resources. This may be in relation to level and skills of staff required to operate the solution or physical elements of the solution. In an IT system, it may be artefacts such as memory, disk capacity, processor power;

- *Security requirements:* These specify the requirements for securing against any threats to the integrity of the solution;

- *Portability requirements:* These specify the need to move the solution from place to place. For example, in an IT solution, this would encompass provision to install software components on other hardware platforms and/ or operating systems;

- *Reliability requirements:* These specify the acceptable mean time between failures of the solution, averaged over a significant period (system availability);

- *Maintainability requirements:* These specify how easy it is to repair faults and adapt the solution to new requirements;

- *Safety requirements*: These specify the requirements to reduce the possibility of causing damage as a direct result of the solution;

- *Recovery requirements*: In an IT solution, these would specify what needs to be done before and after system failure, e.g. backup requirements to enable recovery when needed, business continuity requirements (the minimal service) and full recovery requirements.

Structure of Requirements

Requirement Decomposition
- Feasibility:
  - A very high level set of requirement is established
- Foundations:
  - A high level set of prioritised requirement is established (a PRL)
  - User stories
- Exploration and Engineering:
  - Each requirement may decompose into more detailed requirements.
  - At some point, it may not need to be written down, but evolved as part of iterative development (prototyping)

© TCC   DSATP/7/8

3. Writing a Good Requirement

A good requirement should be clearly stated and should not be in conflict with other requirements within the solution.

3.1 SMART requirements

To develop and document a requirement in a useful and useable way, it is helpful to define it in a **SMART** way, where the acronym signifies that the requirement will be:

Specific

Measurable

Achievable

Realistic

Time-bound

Where the definition relates to a functional requirement it is a useful starting point to begin by stating:

'We need the ability to ...'

And then begin the requirement from that point. For example:

[We need the ability to...] Add a new course delegate.

[We need the ability to...] Accept a payment.

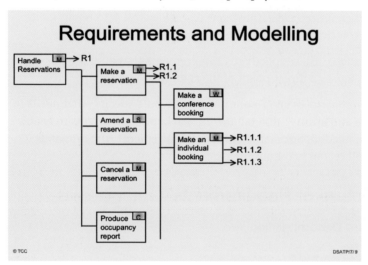

3.2 User stories

A further requirements technique is to think of the requirement as a story related to the way in which it will be used. The construct is:

As a .... (user role)

I need .... (this requirement)

in order to .... (purpose, business value)

For example:

As a   Training Course Administrator

    I need to   Add a new course delegate

        In order to   send them joining instructions

            to attend a training course

            for which they will pay.

Defining the requirement in this way checks it against a business goal (getting people to attend training courses). It also uncovers two other related requirements (send joining instructions; make payment).

3.3 Non-functional requirements

Where the definition relates to a non-functional requirement, the following wording is often useful:

'We know we're successful if ...'

These non-functional requirements are the acceptance criteria for the functional requirements. It is important to build these in as a measure of success and a means of testing that each requirement has been achieved satisfactorily.

A few examples of non-functional requirements are:

- Response times

  '...less than or equal to 2 seconds is optimum; 4 seconds is the worst case acceptable.'

- Security and privacy

  Each transaction may be subject to restrictions on who uses it. This too must be recorded against each requirement, perhaps with a constraint on how it will be implemented:

  '...only accessible to staff of grade 3 and above in the Accounts Department.'

- Availability

  Some systems, particularly business critical and safety critical systems, need to operate without breakdown. Other parts of a system should be available seven days a week, throughout the year during office hours, but there are levels of tolerance in case of a breakdown in service:

  'This service should be available 24/7/365; loss of service for no more than one hour, no more than twice per week can be tolerated.'

Usability should also be specified, with some form of metric, as a non-functional requirement. To say a solution should 'be user-friendly' says nothing useful.

4. Prioritising Requirements and MoSCoW

Delivering on a guaranteed date without compromising quality may mean that some of what was originally envisaged for an individual delivery may have to be left out. However, it is important that essential work is done and that only less critical work is omitted. The key to ensuring that this is the case is the clear prioritisation of the requirements.

4.1 The MoSCoW rules

What is MoSCoW?

Must Have:
- Fundamental to system.
- Without them, system unworkable/useless.
- Minimum usable subset,
- Guaranteed to be developed.

Should Have:
- Important requirements.
- Would be mandatory, but workaround exists
- System will be useful/usable without them.

© TCC

DSATP/7/ 1

The simple MoSCoW rules are used to prioritise what is to be delivered. The acronym MosCoW represents the following levels of requirement priority:

Must Have

These are requirements that are fundamental to the solution. They form the minimum usable subset of requirements which the project must provide to be worthwhile. A good way to check if a requirement is a Must Have is to ask:

'What would happen if we leave that requirement out?'

Typical justifications for Must Have priority are that, without it, the product:

- Won't work / cannot be delivered;

- Is not legal;

- Is unsafe;

- Does not fulfil the business case benefits needed;

- Cannot be deployed, or deployment would be pointless / counterproductive.

Should Have

This category is for those requirements which are very important, but the solution can be useful and usable without them. They are important but not absolutely essential. A good way to check if a requirement is a Should Have is to ask:

'What would happen if we leave that requirement out?'

If the answer is: 'It would be uncomfortable, but we'd cope' then it is definitely not a Must Have. The degree of pain or risk or loss of benefit will determine whether it is then a Should Have or Could Have.

Typical justifications for Should Haves are:

- It may be painful to leave it out, but the solution is still viable and beneficial without it;

- We will lose some business benefit, but the business case still stands, and the project is justified without it;

- There is a work-around, perhaps in the short term, if we leave this out.

What is MoSCoW?

Could Have:
- Would add business benefit
- More easily left out of this increment than Should Haves.

Won't Have this time:
- Valuable requirements, but can wait until a later increment.

Note: All prioritisation is with respect to a clear project objective.

© TCC   DSATP/7/ 1.

Could Have

This category represents requirements that can more easily be left out of the increment being planned. A good way to check if a requirement is a Could Have is to ask:

'What would happen if we leave that requirement out?'

If the answer is: 'It would be disappointing not to get it but it would not actually cause problems', or 'Business benefit would be lost, but not a significant amount, and certainly not enough to jeopardise the business case', then it is a Could Have.

Could Have requirements are:

- Wanted or desirable, but not vital;

- Not such high impact on benefits as Should Haves;

- Less painful to leave out than Should Haves.

Won't Have this time

Won't Haves are valuable requirements that the business have agreed can wait until a later increment, or even a later project. These are still recorded in the Prioritised Requirements List, to act as a record that these have already been agreed as outside of the current scope. At the outset of the project there are unlikely to be many requirements in this category. Won't Haves usually emerge when the project is in progress and, due to time constraints, Could Have or Should Have requirements are de-scoped.

Some requirements might emerge and be immediately classified as Won't Haves. For example, 'I've had a great idea.' 'Yes, that is good but we have not got time to do it now.'

The exact wording for the definitions of the levels of priority associated with MoSCoW should be clarified in relation to each project, to ensure that they make sense in context. These definitions should be agreed with stakeholders before the requirements capture begins, so that definitions can be made objectively.

4.2 The Minimum Usable Subset

The Must Haves form the Minimum Usable Subset; anything less than a Must Have classification means this requirement is not guaranteed. Therefore the

Must Haves alone need to form a coherent solution, without any of the lower priority requirements.

However, it is not intended at the outset that only the Must Haves will be delivered. When planning is done, the M, S and C requirements are all allocated what is estimated to be sufficient time in the plan for their completion. Only the Won't Haves are excluded.

4.3 Effective prioritisation

Priorities should always be decided by an appropriate empowered group of stakeholders, with reference to the project objective and the Business Case. It is within the Business Analyst's remit to challenge the priorities and within the power of the Business Sponsor, Business Visionary and Business Ambassadors to justify the prioritisations.

The MoSCoW rules provide the basis on which decisions are made about the priorities to which the Solution Development Team will work during the whole project and during any Timebox within the project. High level requirements and their priorities are agreed and baselined at the end of the Foundations phase. However, priorities may be reassessed based on an increased understanding as the project progresses. They may also alter in a changing business environment. Therefore, priorities remain under review and are continually re-assessed to confirm that they are still valid. As new requirements arise during a project, or as existing requirements are defined in more detail, MoSCoW prioritisation of the new elements will be needed.

It is important that there is an ongoing plan for development beyond the present increment or project. It is very hard to obtain any flexibility in prioritisation when a project has budget for only one increment. In those circumstances, everything is a Must Have!

It is essential that not every feature is a Must Have. If everything to be achieved within the project, within an increment or within any development Timebox, is a Must Have, there is no flexibility to bring the project back on track if problems arise. It is the de-scoping of these lower priority requirements that enables teams to deliver on time when problems arise.

Metrics should be kept, for each development Timebox, regarding the proportion of Should Have and Could Have requirements being delivered, in order to have an ongoing predictive estimate of the likely percentage delivery of the whole project.

The Requirement Lifecycle

Each Requirement must be subject to:

- Elicitation
  - Workshops, model-building, interviews, observation, scenarios
- Analysis
  - Realistic? Ambiguous? Combination of Requirements? Aligned with Business?
- Validation
  - Prototypes, reviews, models, testing
- Management
  - Traceability, stability, Change Management

5. The Lifecycle of a Requirement

Any requirement passes through four lifecycle stages:

- Elicitation – the requirement is identified via a recognised fact-finding technique such as interview, observation or workshop;

- Analysis – the requirement is analysed to determine if it is realistic, ambiguous in any way or conflicting with other requirements;

- Validation – the requirement is validated by review or by examination of the models of the system;

- Management – the requirement has to be documented, and modifications and further sub-division of the requirement have to be recorded.

6. Structure of a Requirement

Requirements are identified at various levels of detail, from a high-level strategic viewpoint through to a more detailed, implementable viewpoint.

High level requirements can be decomposed into sub-requirements which can be further sub-divided into even more detailed requirements.

It is the very nature of this decomposition that can help resolve one of the problems which may be confronted by the team. If all of the requirements seem to be 'Must Haves', it may be that they are still at too high a level. Further decomposition of the requirement may produce sub-requirements amongst which 'Should Have' and 'Could Have' requirements can be found.

7. The Prioritised Requirements List (PRL)

As requirements are being elicited, existing ones modified and new ones added, a list of requirements for the new system is built up.

The Prioritised Requirements List contains the definition of each requirement. A suggested structure for each requirement definition is:

- Requirement ID;

- Requirement short name;

- Requirement description;

- Function / feature which it is a part of;

- Acceptance criteria;

- Priority (MoSCoW);

- Timebox;

- Effort required;

- Owner;

- Sign-off – who and how;

- Dependency on other requirements;

- Business benefit (high, medium, low).

Other information may be added, depending on the project type.

The Prioritised Requirements List defines both functional and non-functional requirements. It is used to plan the contents of development Timeboxes.

8. Conclusion

A requirement is a service or function that a user wishes the solution provided by the project to perform, or a feature that the solution should exhibit. There are two categories of requirement: functional and non-functional.

Requirements should be expressed along with their acceptance criteria from the outset: high level requirements have high level acceptance criteria.

The MoSCoW rules are used to prioritise what is to be delivered. The Must Haves form the minimum usable subset of the solution.

Requirements are elicited, analysed, validated and managed throughout the project. The Prioritised Requirements List forms the high-level baseline of agreed requirements, from which the project's development Timeboxes are planned.

Requirements Definition and Prioritisation

1. **What does the 'W' in MoSCoW stand for?**

   A} Want to have this time

   B} Won't have this time

   C} Would Have

   D} Would Like

2. **A Functional Requirement describes:**

   A} What the final product will do

   B} How well the final product will work

   C} When the final product will be ready

   D} Whether the final product will be maintainable

3. **A Non-Functional Requirement may describe:**

   A} The performance aspects of the solution

   B} The features contained in the solution

   C} The users of each feature

   D} How long each functional requirement will take to develop

4. **The lifecycle stages of a requirement are:**

   A} Elicitation, Analysis, Validation, Management

   B} Exploration, Engineering, Deployment, Management

   C} Exploration, Analysis, Design, Test

   D} Elicitation, Engineering, Management, Deployment

5. **The Must Have requirements:**

   A} Will always be delivered before any Should Haves or Could Haves

   B} Will be the first priority if nothing better comes along

   C} Are the minimum usable subset of the project's requirements

   D} Represent the unreasonable demands of the business, and they cannot expect to get them all

Answers can be found on page 222

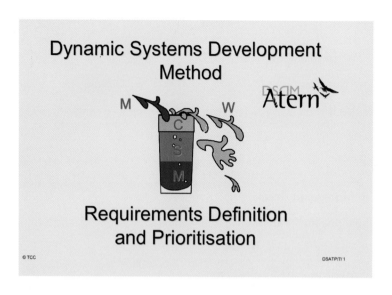

What is a Requirement?

In simple terms, a requirement is a:

- Feature
- Function
- Service
- Constraint

...that the solution needs to perform or exhibit

DSATP/7/4

Defining the Requirements

- Define a requirement along with its Acceptance Criteria as measurable targets at all levels.

- Give it a unique ID

- Keep details of:
  - Source
  - Owner
  - Business benefit
  - Priority
  - Other?

DSATP/7/5

Functional Requirements

- Functional Requirement is "what", not "how"

- Make it SMART
  - Specific
  - Measurable
  - Achievable
  - Realistic
  - Timely

- Wording - Functional Requirement:
  - "We need the ability to ..."
  - "As a ... I need ... in order to ..."

- Not in conflict with, or overlapping, other requirements

DSATP/7/6

Non-Functional Requirements

- Non-Functional Requirements are about "**How well**" we do the Functional Requirements, i.e. with what:

  - Security
  - Availability
  - Portability
  - Maintainability

  - External interfaces
  - Design constraints
  - Performance
  - Response time
  - etc. (see notes)

- May be global or related to just one Functional Requirement

- May need extra time in the plan!

Structure of Requirements

Requirement Decomposition

- Feasibility:
  - A very high level set of requirement is established
- Foundations:
  - A high level set of prioritised requirement is established (a PRL)
  - User stories
- Exploration and Engineering:
  - Each requirement may decompose into more detailed requirements.
  - At some point, it may not need to be written down, but evolved as part of iterative development (prototyping)

Requirements and Modelling

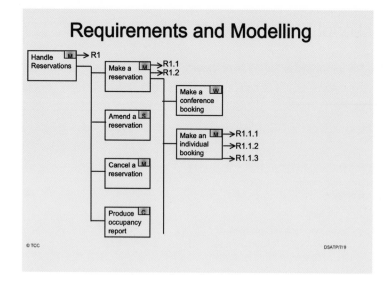

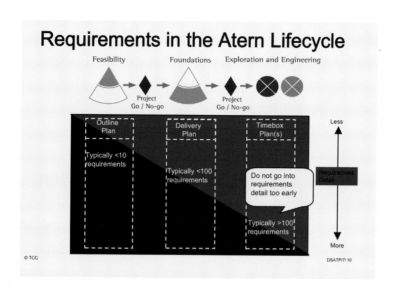

What is MoSCoW?

Must Have:
- Fundamental to system.
- Without them, system unworkable/useless.
- Minimum usable subset,
- Guaranteed to be developed.

Should Have:
- Important requirements.
- Would be mandatory, but workaround exists
- System will be useful/usable without them.

DSATP/7/11

What is MoSCoW?

Could Have:
- Would add business benefit
- More easily left out of this increment than Should Haves.

Won't Have this time:
- Valuable requirements, but can wait until a later increment.

Note: All prioritisation is with respect to a clear project objective.

DSATP/7/12

The Requirement Lifecycle

Each Requirement must be subject to:

- Elicitation
  - Workshops, model-building, interviews, observation, scenarios
- Analysis
  - Realistic? Ambiguous? Combination of Requirements? Aligned with Business?
- Validation
  - Prototypes, reviews, models, testing
- Management
  - Traceability, stability, Change Management

Session Summary

- What is a Requirement?

- Functional and Non-functional Requirements

- Requirements in the Atern lifecycle

- Requirements and modelling

- The Requirement lifecycle

Dynamic Systems Development Method

Atern

Requirements Definition and Prioritisation

8. Iterative Development and Prototyping

1. Introduction

Iterative Development is a key technique of DSDM Atern. It is the approach used to evolve a solution from the high level objective to a delivered product. Iterative Development is intrinsically bound up with Prototyping. Prototypes, mock ups and models can be used to establish requirements, confirm expectations and test the achievability and achievement of those objectives. In this chapter we explore both Iterative Development and Prototyping.

2. What is a Prototype?

A prototype is something that serves to illustrate the typical qualities of the eventual solution. It may evolve into the eventual solution (an evolutionary prototype) or may always be intended to be an experimental model (a disposable prototype).

A prototype in Atern is a piece of work that demonstrates how a given objective can be or has been achieved.

2.1 Disposable prototypes

An example of a disposable ('throw away') prototype in an IT-based solution is the Architectural Spike, also known as a Proof of Concept prototype, which is a thin, end-to-end mock-up of the pathway through a solution. It may be created in order to explore options and work out the best way forward. DSDM Atern calls these Capability/Technique prototypes.

An example of a disposable prototype for a building project would be the one-ten-thousandth size scale model of the building complex, often displayed in the foyer of the finished building, under glass!

2.2 Evolutionary prototypes

All Iterative Development on a particular deliverable, carried out in accordance with the Iterative Development cycle described in Section 3, can be considered to be Prototyping, because elements are constantly being built, shown, modified and revisited. For this reason, the whole Iterative Development technique is sometimes referred to as Prototyping.

2.3 Benefits of building prototypes

The benefits of building prototypes are significant. Prototyping is one of the many ways by which DSDM Atern ensures effective communication between stakeholders, whether from different parts of the business, different organisations or sometimes different cultures, languages and/or countries. DSDM Atern advocates the use of models to improve communication and to make ideas and developing products visible.

Early Prototyping may involve diagrammatic representations of the analysis or design work for the project. In a building project, blueprints are drawn of the design; for an electrical product, a circuit diagram is constructed. Prototyping in DSDM Atern is about collaboratively evolving diagrams, pictures, models and working software that help to define the problem or the intended solution. The intention is to produce something visible, valuable and working as soon as possible, since this is less open to interpretation than textual or diagrammatic representations of a solution. Only then is it possible for the intended users of the solution to say if what has been produced is what they actually need.

3. Iterative Development

Iterative Development is a key technique which is a fundamental way of working in a DSDM Atern project. It allows the high-level requirements established during the Foundations phase to be explored and evolved in more detail during the Development Timeboxes of Exploration and Engineering. It ensures that the cycles of iteration in the Development Timeboxes are controlled, and that a feedback loop is built into the way of working within these Timeboxes.

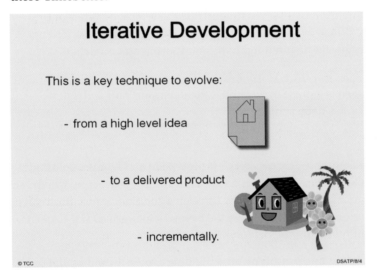

Iterative Development cycles are short, typically a matter of days or even hours. The steps within the cycle are:

- *Identify:* The team agree the objective of the current work;

- *Plan:* The team work out what needs to be done, by whom, to meet that objective;

- *Evolve:* The team work on the solution;

- *Review:* The work is tested to see if the objective has been achieved.

If the review shows that the objective was not met, the Solution Development Team may:

- Discard the changes and revert to the last agreed version of the product;

- Identify the work required for the objective to be achieved.

The feedback afforded by the cycle ensures that the solution evolves, over time, in a controlled manner.

Note: these cycles are based on the control cycle defined by W Edwards Deming – The Deming Cycle is 'Plan – Do – Check – Act' (PDCA).

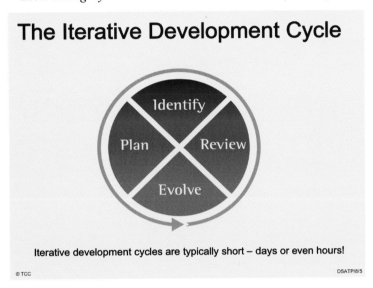

3.1 Iterative Development of the Evolving Solution

The product of a DSDM Atern project is evolved over time to accommodate specific functional and non-functional requirements, captured in the Prioritised Requirements List.

At any given time, the Iterative Development cycle may focus on evolving the solution from one or more of the following perspectives:

- *Functional perspective* – demonstrating how a business functionality has been achieved;

- *Usability perspective* – demonstrating how the user of the solution interacts with it to achieve the business objective (this category of non-functional requirement is singled out for special attention because the user-view of the way the solution drives the evolutionary development approach);

- *Non-functional perspective* – demonstrating how general issues related to, for example, performance, capacity, security or maintainability have been accommodated.

3.2 Managing the Iterative Development process

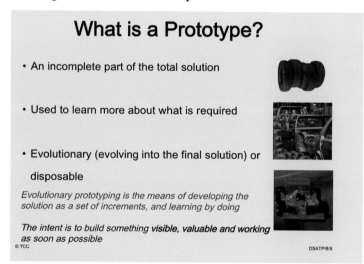

Perspectives for Iterative Development

- Functional

- Usability

- Non-functional
  (e.g. performance & capacity)

Management of the Iterative Development process is achieved through:

- Timeboxing;

- Change Control (in association with MoSCoW prioritisation);

- Configuration Management;

- Quality assurance and testing.

Successful Iterative Development is very dependent on continual and frequent involvement and feedback from the business roles, and on collaborative working of the Solution Development Team.

What is a Prototype?

- An incomplete part of the total solution

- Used to learn more about what is required

- Evolutionary (evolving into the final solution) or disposable

Evolutionary prototyping is the means of developing the solution as a set of increments, and learning by doing

The intent is to build something visible, valuable and working as soon as possible

© TCC   DSATP/8/8

Development Timeboxes should follow the structure below:

Kick-off
In the kick-off session at the start of the Timebox, the team plans how to work on the requirements identified for that Timebox.

Iteration
DSDM Atern then recommends three iterations:

- *Investigation*: This involves a single pass through the Iterative Development cycle, identifying products to be evolved in the Timebox and gaining a detailed understanding of the requirements to be addressed and solutions to be created. Typically, Investigation takes 10% to 20% of the total Development Timebox time.

- *Refinement:* This relates to most of the work of the Timebox, with the evolutionary activity being driven by the MoSCoW priorities established in the Prioritised Requirements List and at the Timebox kick-off. Typically, Refinement takes 60% to 80% of the total Development Timebox time.

- *Consolidation:* Relates to the work to fully complete as many of the planned deliverables as possible within the Development Timebox, in accordance with MoSCoW priorities. Typically, Consolidation takes 10% to 20% of the total Development Timebox time.

Once Consolidation is complete, at the end of the Timebox, one further step is Close Out.

Iterative Development – Functional Perspective

- Focuses on functionality
- Developer demonstrates **functional business requirements**
- **This checks developer's understanding of user requirements**
- **Confirms 'building the right solution'**

© TCC   DSATP/8/10

Close Out

At Close Out, the Solution Development Team and the Project Manager review what has been achieved, against the objectives of the Timebox. Anything planned for delivery but not completed within the Timebox has to be addressed. It may become a Won't Have, by agreement between the Solution Development Team; it may be included in a later Timebox, but something else may need to be de-scoped to include this. If Must Have requirements have not been completed, re-planning to include these in exchange for later Could Have or Should Have requirements needs to be done. The impact on the overall project delivery date must be assessed. If delivery on time of the Must Haves is threatened, this is an issue for escalation to the Business Sponsor.

3.3 Planning the Development Timeboxes

By the end of Foundations, there will be a Prioritised Requirements List (PRL) with MoSCoW priorities embedded in it.

This is used to plan the Timeboxes for Exploration and Engineering.

At this stage, the Solution Development Team needs to decide the overall approach to the development and delivery of the solution. This information becomes part of the Delivery Plan.

Three approaches are:

- Vertical;

- Horizontal;

- Combined.

Vertical Approach

This approach delivers thin vertical slices of the working solution, for example just one function or feature of the end solution. As more vertical slices are completed, they can be integrated with previously completed functionality. A Vertical Approach is a good choice where the solution is to be delivered incrementally. Together with the Combined Approach, this is probably the most commonly used approach in DSDM Atern projects.

- *Advantage:* The project can deliver something useful early;

- *Disadvantage:* It may be difficult to see the context of the delivery.

Horizontal Approach

This approach delivers the solution layer by layer. The layers could be functional or architectural. A Horizontal Approach should be chosen where the solution can naturally be viewed and developed in layers. The Horizontal Approach is probably the least commonly used approach.

- *Advantage:* If a user interface slice is chosen first, it can be used to give an early demonstration of the look and feel of a solution;

- *Disadvantage:* Nothing usable is completed until the final Timebox.

A Combined Approach

This approach starts by delivering a (thin) end-to-end slice of the solution (Horizontal), and then reverts to a Vertical Approach to deliver complete working pieces of the solution which fit into the high level solution framework. A Combined Approach is useful to confirm the end-to-end scope before getting into the detail of the individual requirements.

- *Advantage:* Early in the project, a single layer of the solution is built (normally the user interface), to demonstrate the end-to-end requirement and to give a clear view of the full extent of the proposed solution. This then provides a framework and clear context for subsequent development/delivery of individual requirements;

- *Disadvantage:* It may take longer to deliver the first usable piece of functionality.

3.4 Iterative Development and Prototyping during the DSDM Atern Lifecycle

The use of Iterative Development and Prototyping practices is embedded in the DSDM Atern lifecycle.

In Pre-Project, it would be possible to construct a prototype to assist in defining the Terms of Reference, but this is more likely to be left to Feasibility.

In Feasibility, a capability/technique prototype could be used to ascertain the practicality of continuing with the project; a functional perspective could be constructed at a very high level to establish key features; a usability perspective may be established here, but this is more likely to be left until later phases unless the risk related to usability is high.

In Foundations, a capability/technique prototype could be used to establish the practicality of following a particular option for solution. The business perspective could be established and prototyped at a high level to demonstrate key features and establish the complexity of what is required, for estimating and Timebox planning purposes; a usability perspective could possibly be constructed, again if the risk in this area is high.

In Exploration, the detailed elements of the evolving solution are being built using Iterative Development within Development Timeboxes. A functional perspective is the main focus to establish the detail of each feature being investigated.

In Engineering, non-functional, and usability perspectives are the main focus, although much of the functional perspective will usually have been established during Exploration. A capability/technique prototype may still be useful here, to prove the concept of more detailed technical approaches.

In Deployment, most of the prototyping should have already been completed. A focus on the usability and non-functional perspectives may still be relevant in the fine-tuning of the solution during Deployment.

In Post-Project, functional, non-functional and usability perspectives form the measures against which benefits realisation is assessed.

4. Conclusion

Iterative Development is one of DSDM Atern's key techniques. The cycles of Identify, Plan, Evolve and Review, combined with the Timebox structure of Investigate, Refine and Consolidate ensure that the iterative process retains all the benefits of evolving a solution through team collaboration whilst, at the same time, ensuring sufficient structure and control.

DSDM Atern also highlights the various options available on planning how the solution may be delivered, Horizontally, Vertically or by a Combined Approach. Within the control of Iterative Development, a Prototyping approach is about collaboratively evolving diagrams, pictures, models and working software that help to define the problem or to build the evolving solution. The aim is to produce something visible, valuable and working as soon as possible.

Iterative Development and Prototyping

1. **What is the objective of iterative development in DSDM Atern?**

   A} To keep the scope entirely flexible

   B} To evolve solutions from a high level idea to a delivered product

   C} To ensure the Business Visionary gets everything they want

   D} To evolve solutions from a blank sheet to a delivered product

2. **On which specific perspectives does DSDM Atern focus during iterative development (prototyping)?**

   A} Performance and capability

   B} Response times, security and maintainability

   C} Process, user interaction and performance

   D} Business, usability, and performance/capacity and capability/technique

3. **Iterative Development is:**

   A} One of the five key techniques in DSDM Atern

   B} Not allowed in DSDM Atern

   C} The only technique in DSDM Atern

   D} An alternative to DSDM Atern

4. **Iterative Development allows the high-level requirements established during the Foundations phase to be:**

   A} Explored and evolved in more detail during the Development Timeboxes

   B} Kept at a high level

   C} Frozen until Deployment

   D} Prioritised by the Solution Tester

5. **The steps within the Iterative Development cycle are:**

   A} Investigate, Review, Consolidate, Close

   B} Identify, Plan, Evolve, Review

   C} Plan, Do, Check, Act

   D} Evolve, Review, Plan, End

Answers can be found on page 222

Dynamic Systems Development Method

Atern

Iterative Development

INVESTIGATION REFINEMENT CONSOLIDATION
KICK OFF CLOSE OUT

Prototyping

Session Objectives

- Iterative Development

- Prototyping

- Evolutionary Development Strategies

Atern 5 Key Techniques

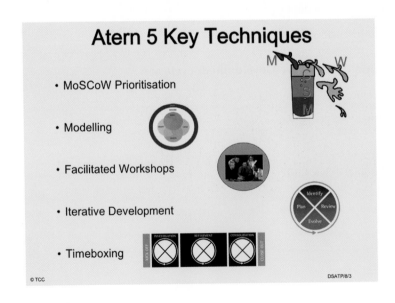

- MoSCoW Prioritisation

- Modelling

- Facilitated Workshops

- Iterative Development

- Timeboxing

© TCC

DSATP/8/3

Iterative Development

This is a key technique to evolve:

- from a high level idea

- to a delivered product

- incrementally.

The Iterative Development Cycle

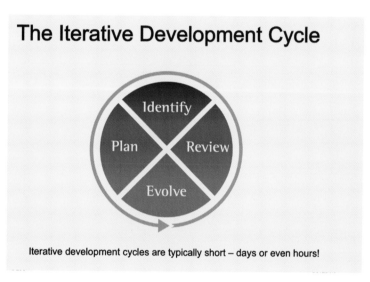

Iterative development cycles are typically short – days or even hours!

Iterative Development in a Timebox

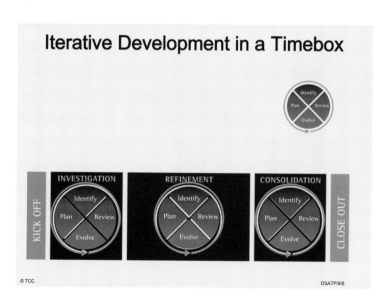

Perspectives for Iterative Development

- Functional

- Usability

- Non-functional
  (e.g. performance & capacity)

What is a Prototype?

- An incomplete part of the total solution

- Used to learn more about what is required

- Evolutionary (evolving into the final solution) or

  disposable

*Evolutionary prototyping is the means of developing the
solution as a set of increments, and learning by doing*

*The intent is to build something visible, valuable and working
as soon as possible*

© TCC

DSATP/8/8

A Few Ideas for Prototyping

Screen-based,
animated

Experimental

Role-play

Paper-based
"low-tech"

Video

© TCC

DSATP/8/9

Iterative Development – Functional Perspective

- Focuses on functionality
- Developer demonstrates functional business requirements
- This checks developer's understanding of user requirements
- Confirms 'building the right solution'

© TCC

DSATP/8/10

Iterative Development – Usability Perspective

- Focuses on user interface
- Illustrates solution ease of use
- User tests ease of use of the solution

Iterative Development – Non-Functional Perspective

- Focuses on non-functional aspects (response time, security etc.)
- Solution Developer tests that the solution meets non-functional requirements

Capability/Technique Prototype

- Focuses on technical design options and functionality

- Solution Developer tests design approach and/or development tool

This is often an **Architectural Spike** or **Proof of Concept**

Evolutionary Development Strategies

Vertical, Horizontal & Combined Approaches

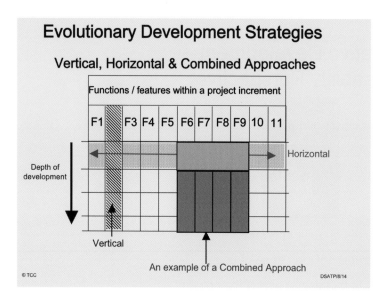

Functions / features within a project increment

| F1 | | F3 | F4 | F5 | F6 | F7 | F8 | F9 | 10 | 11 |

Depth of development

Horizontal

Vertical

An example of a Combined Approach

© TCC

DSATP/8/14

Session Summary

- Iterative Development

- Prototyping

- Evolutionary Development Strategies

Dynamic Systems Development Method

Iterative Development

Prototyping

9. Estimating and Timeboxing

1. Estimating

An estimate is a forecast of how much of the following it is expected to take to deliver a specific requirement or objective:

- Cost;
- Effort;
- Skills;
- Person hours of time;
- Elapsed time.

Alternatively:

- An estimate could be a forecast of how much functionality can be delivered for a given cost, effort, skills, time.

The underlying purpose of estimating is normally:

- To assess project feasibility and justification by evaluating costs and benefits (Business Case);
- To assist project planning, scheduling and control.

Associated with each estimate should be a statement of assumptions and risks.

An estimate is only a prediction, based on information available at the time. This should be clear to all stakeholders; since there is the uncertainty of an unknown future, and the requirements are at a high level when initial estimates are made, and the actual effort required will almost certainly be different.

For estimating in DSDM Atern there are four key points:

- Estimates need to include a level of contingency to cover the risk associated with unknown factors. In DSDM Atern, contingency is found in the Should Have and Could Have requirements;
- Estimates need *just* enough precision and accuracy for their purpose at that point in the lifecycle. Over-precise estimates can be misleading;
- Estimates should be made by those who will be responsible for developing and delivering the product;

- Estimates should be revisited and refined throughout the project.

1.1 Estimating within the DSDM Atern lifecycle

Estimating is done throughout the DSDM Atern project. It is recommended that estimates are revisited at the start of each Timebox.

- *Pre-Project:* Before the project begins, estimates are based on scant information. They may often be of the form:

    - this is the objective;

    - this is the money we have;

    - this is the time we have.

The Estimating Process

There are a number of distinct steps:

- Estimate the effort required

- Adjust the effort for environmental factors

- Identify the products and their inter-dependencies

- Schedule the product deliveries and allocate resource

- Adjust the schedule in the light of known constraints

© TCC   DSATP/9/8

It is more a set of constraints than an estimate.

Early estimates give a broad picture, sufficient only to support the decision whether or not to proceed. Initial estimates should be validated and revised to give increasing accuracy based on emerging detail:

- *Feasibility:* Here the first estimate for the duration of the whole project is made. The purpose of the estimate is to assess the practicality of the project in terms of cost and to develop an outline plan. Initial estimates during Feasibility will be based on the limited information known about the project at this stage, but also on experience of similar solutions and projects.

- *Foundations:* At this point, a more detailed estimate for the whole project is made. The project will now have been scoped, and a prioritised set of requirements will be available. The definition of resources available will permit planning of Timeboxes and the presentation of a Timeboxed Delivery Plan with Must Have, Should Have and Could Have requirements planned in. In a commercial environment, estimates at this point often form the basis for a contract. Therefore, estimates must reflect the level of risk and confidence acceptable to the stakeholders. The Should Have and Could Have requirements are understood at this point to represent contingency.

- *Exploration and Engineering:* The estimate from Foundations forms the basis for the whole project. However, estimates will be monitored and refined throughout Exploration and Engineering, for each Timebox. The focus will be on meeting objectives within the Timeboxes rather than amending Timebox deadlines, and on completing at least the Must Haves, although time has been allowed in Timeboxes for Should Haves and Could Haves.

- *Deployment:* The Deployment Plan is prepared during Exploration and Engineering. Before this, estimates for the Deployment Phase are only possible at a high level.

In DSDM Atern, the Solution Development Team should be involved in estimating the work they are to do, since they are best able to assess what they will be able to achieve. Additionally, if they agree to tight timescales, they are more likely to buy-in to achieving these if they have been involved in the estimates than if they have had the timescales imposed upon them. If the estimates have to be made by parties outside the team, the team must be encouraged to confirm that the timescales are realistic.

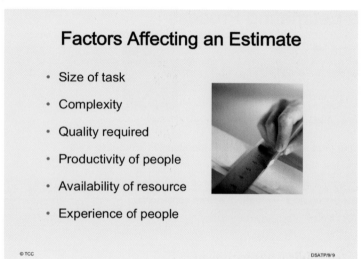

Factors Affecting an Estimate

- Size of task
- Complexity
- Quality required
- Productivity of people
- Availability of resource
- Experience of people

© TCC   DSATP/9/9

1.2   Contingency

A traditional project management approach would agree to deliver all of a set of features and would accept that time and cost may vary. Tolerances may be set to restrict how much variance is acceptable. Quality may inadvertently vary.

DSDM Atern projects fix cost, time and quality and look for their contingency in the de-scoping of less-important features.

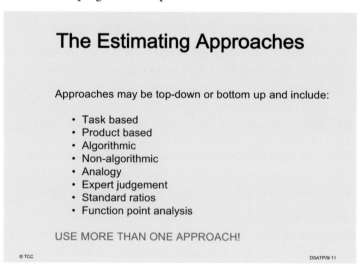

The Estimating Approaches

Approaches may be top-down or bottom up and include:

- Task based
- Product based
- Algorithmic
- Non-algorithmic
- Analogy
- Expert judgement
- Standard ratios
- Function point analysis

USE MORE THAN ONE APPROACH!

© TCC   DSATP/9/11

Thus, contingency in a DSDM Atern project is managed by the prioritisation of the features rather than by adding extra time or cost. Contingency is built into estimates and is not an additional percentage of tolerance.

As a rule of thumb, Must Haves should not constitute more than 60% of the project effort. If the project risk is high, even this may be too much to guarantee on-time delivery of the minimum usable subset.

1.3   DSDM Atern top 10 estimating tips

- Use early estimates to support decisions, but do not expect them to be definitive and unchanging. An estimate giving a range is more appropriate than a single value at this point;

- Ensure there are sufficient Should Haves and Could Haves to provide contingency;

- Estimates should be carried out by, and belong to, those who will be doing the work;

- Use a collaborative approach to produce estimates;

- Challenge all estimates – either by using more than one approach to give a comparison, or by taking input from a range of individuals;

- Estimate based on the knowledge available at the time. High level requirements can only give rise to high level estimates;

- Estimates should be directly related to business requirements;

- Document all estimates, detailing scope, assumptions, calculations and risks;

- Collect metrics to validate and improve estimates;

- Learn from experience.

Why are Estimates Wrong?

- Inexperience of estimating

- Doing something that has not been done before

- Inadequate techniques

- Optimistic assumptions

- Wrong person making estimates

- Lack of information

© TCC   DSATP/9/12

1.4   The estimating process

The estimating process has a number of distinct elements:

- Estimate the effort required; this involves assessing the size of the project as a whole, or sizing its component parts and estimating the effort required to deliver each;

- Adjust the effort for environmental factors; assess the estimate against reality, cross-checking;

- Identify the products and the dependencies between them;

- Schedule the product deliveries and allocate resource;

- Adjust the schedule in the light of known constraints (time for example).

There are two approaches to estimating, *top down* and *bottom up*.

Top down techniques (e.g. estimating by analogy to a similar project):
- Are based on the business requirements (rather than system components);

- Give a figure for the project as a whole;

- Are fast to prepare;

- Can be derived from high-level requirements;

- Give a high-level view of the project which can be used to evaluate feasibility.

Bottom up techniques:
- Are based on tangible solution components;

- Give detailed estimates for low-level components;

- Are time-consuming to prepare;

- Need detailed knowledge of likely system components;

- Provide a good basis for project planning and scheduling.

The use of both types of estimating approach allows the team to calibrate the estimates for a particular type / size of project within a specific development environment. This should provide more accurate estimates of project resource costs.

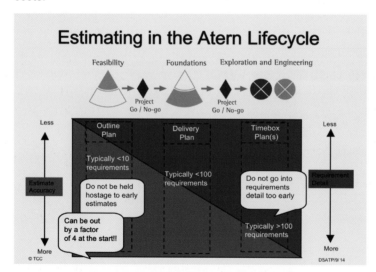

1.5   Approaches to estimating

The discussion which follows is not specifically DSDM Atern-related but provides a collection of approaches for illustrative purposes.

The following approaches, whilst not exhaustive, illustrate the variety which are available:

- *Task based*: This is based upon tasks or activities which will be performed during the project. It is relevant where the method to be used in the project is strongly task-oriented. Task based estimating is easier where initial estimates are required;

- *Product based:* Product deliverables are the basic unit for estimating and it is particularly appropriate where the method is strongly orientated toward product definition;

- *Algorithmic:* The algorithmic approach is used to eliminate the subjective judgements that must be made in estimating. It uses historical data on past projects (industry standard or organisation specific) which have been adjusted for the specific project environment. Formulae are used to calculate the estimates for the project;

- *Non-algorithmic:* This covers a whole raft of ploys for estimating, from a largely intuitive approach through to a disciplined method. The more that it draws upon historical data, the more accurate the estimate is likely to be;

- *Analogy:* This is the experience route to an estimate. If an individual has performed a particular task before then they will be better placed to estimate a similar future task. Expert tools for estimating will capture this information for re-use. Obviously analogy will rely upon an accurate comparison between the project and other historical projects, the accuracy of the estimate which is produced being dependent upon the 'goodness of fit'. For this reason some adjustment may be required to compensate for any differences. Analogy is particularly appropriate in the early stages of the project where only the broad characteristics of the project are known, with very little detail being available;

- *Expert judgement:* Here the knowledge and expertise of individuals are used to obtain estimates based on previous experience. Experienced project managers who have worked on similar projects in the past may provide these estimates. Such estimates give a top down approach to estimating the whole project. The approach may also be implemented using experts in particular activities to provide estimates on distinct areas of the project, their estimates then being combined to produce an estimate for the whole project;

- *Standard ratios:* Standard percentage ratios for the various stages of a project are applied. Once a firm estimate has been made upon an early stage, the ratios can then be applied to provide an estimate for future stages and the project as a whole;

- *Function Point Analysis:* This is a top down algorithmic approach which uses some known key features of the solution to derive a Function Point Index (FPI) for it, weighted for the technical complexity of the project. The FPI is then applied against productivity figures to derive an estimate.

1.6 Pitfalls of estimating

One salutary warning: estimates have a tendency to become self-fulfilling since the estimate is used to define the project budget with the consequence that the project is adjusted to meet the budgetary figure.

1.7 Workshops for estimating

One of the best ways to achieve agreement on estimates for a DSDM Atern project is to hold a Facilitated Workshop, where those who will be responsible for delivery of the project make the estimates. This approach gains commitment and ownership of the estimates, and takes account of team skills and capabilities. This approach may be used for estimating Development Timeboxes. It can also be used in early estimates (during Feasibility and Foundations) where the workshop participants are selected for their relevant technical and business knowledge. Someone with independent estimating skills may also be included.

1.8 Presenting the estimate

Early project estimates are best presented as a range, to indicate the level of confidence of the estimate; early estimates cannot be precise to an exact figure. If the basis of information for the estimate is high, then figures should be rounded to a level that properly reflects this level of impreciseness. An estimate of the best and worst cases may also be appropriate, taking risk into account.

1.9 Completing the estimate

Some factors to consider are:

- Does the Solution Development Team have the right level of the appropriate skills? Learning curves are expensive;

- Are the team members exclusively available to this project? Time is lost in switching between tasks and there may be other activities the team members have to do during the project (administration, career management, other projects, holidays);

- Have all activities been included in the estimates, such as administration and preparation for Workshops, project and team management, communications, reviews, meetings;

- Do estimates take account of delivery approach, parallel working, incremental delivery and the requirements for post deployment support of increments whilst still working on the next increment;

- Do project costs take account of the practical allocation of team members, lease of buildings, provision of office facilities, hardware and third party services.

1.10 Reviewing the estimates

Estimates should always be challenged by independent review and / or by using more than one approach. A team approach to estimating has a built-in level of review, but it is still valuable to have an independent check. This is most important with early project estimates, which are based on limited information and experience.

1.11 Summary of estimating

An estimate is not just a number. It must be supported with enough information to be able to justify it, refine it, qualify it and repeat it. This includes a statement of:

- Scope;

- Assumptions;

- Dependencies;

- Detail of how it was arrived at (calculations);

- Source information on which it was based;

- Risks to its reliability;

- The estimating approach used;

- Any other related documents.

It is often useful to provide a degree of confidence in the estimate based on the level of information on which it was based. The level of documentation must be appropriate to the project; enough to meet project needs at the point in the lifecycle to which it relates and no more.

2. Timeboxing

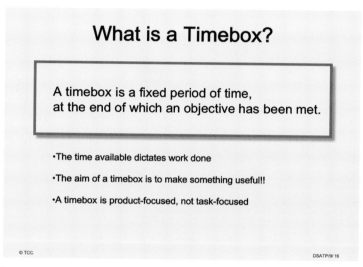

"*Creative people in many walks of life have a deadline. A magazine writer, television producer or seminar developer creates material for a certain date. Whatever else happens, they must not fail to meet the deadline.*

To meet the deadline, they may allow the contents to slip. There may be items they want to include but cannot do so in time. The producer of a television documentary or a seminar broadcast by satellite may say 'I wish I could have interviewed so-and-so' or 'I wish we had better footage on this'. However, there is no time to obtain the extra interview or footage. The deadline is absolute. The show must go on the air. There is much similarity between television production and the building of information systems. Television production employs a planning phase, design and storyboarding, then construction. A difference is that most information system (IS) development does not have a firm deadline. Sometimes developers claim for a year that the system is '95%' complete."

JAMES MARTIN

2.1 Introduction to Timeboxing

Timeboxing is a key technique in DSDM Atern. The purpose of Timeboxing is to control the amount of time taken to complete a piece of work, and to maximise the effectiveness of the effort spent.

It is more than just a mechanism for partitioning development work into small chunks. It is a well-defined process with review points and checks on the quality of products produced.

Here we shall look at the key characteristics of Timeboxing, the main project management requirements for success, and a recommended approach to Timeboxing.

2.2 What is a Timebox?

A Timebox is a fixed period of time, at the end of which an objective has been met. The objective will be a deliverable of some sort.

The aim of a Timebox is to make something which is complete and tested. A Timebox is product-based, rather than task-based.

Timeboxing is an essential aspect of DSDM Atern projects. It allows the iterative nature of the work to be controlled and deliverables to be produced on time and to the right quality.

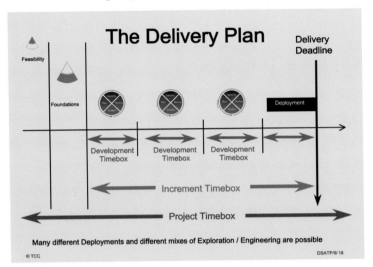

Timeboxing is a process by which defined objectives are reached at a pre-determined and immovable date by invoking the agreed flexibility of requirements and using MoSCoW prioritisation.

There are various levels at which Timeboxing takes place within DSDM Atern projects:

- From project start to project end-date forms a Project Timebox. The end-date is fixed and the business objectives to be achieved by that date are defined;

- Each delivery increment in a project can be defined as an Increment Timebox. The end-date for an increment is fixed and the prioritised requirements (business and technical) to be satisfied by that date are defined;

- An early phase within the lifecycle may be defined as a Timebox. e.g. Feasibility, Foundations;

- Development Timeboxes may be defined, particularly during Exploration and Engineering, for the work of evolving and prototyping pieces of the solution;

- A workshop or review session will often be defined as a Timeboxed event, with a fixed start and end time and predefined products.

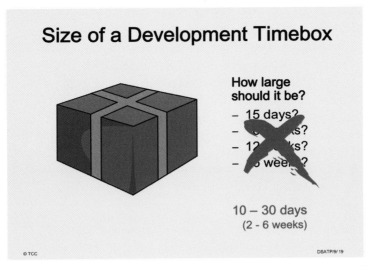

Development Timeboxes are typically between 10 and 30 days (two to six weeks) in length: the shorter the better. However these limits are not mandatory. A major advantage of keeping Timeboxes short is that the amount of work to be achieved within a Timebox is smaller and therefore estimates of the effort required are likely to be more accurate. Additionally, failing to meet a deadline on a short Timebox near the beginning of the project gives an early warning for the deadlines of the project, at a point where action can be taken to correct this.

2.3 Reasons for Timeboxing

Timeboxing was first reportedly used by Du Pont Fibres, who made a management decision to restrict their development cycles to 90 working days (four months). If a project was seen to be larger than this, it would be broken into smaller increments. (They later extended this to 120 days, six months, to allow time for project close-down and documentation completion.)

Timeboxing prevents the 'creeping functionality' often found in iterative prototyping situations and the tendency of the development not to converge towards a working solution. It prevents the '95% complete' syndrome where, from the point in time when Solution Developers feel that their development is '95% complete', it takes as long again to actually complete!

3. Timebox Planning

3.1 Order of Timeboxes

The order of work within the Development Timeboxes should be driven by the business requirements for the increment and also by the need for architectural components to be in place on which to build the functionality. It will also be governed by the risks identified for the project.

Early Timeboxes should address high priority business functionality, architectural components and also the areas where there is least confidence in the time / effort estimates.

3.2 Examining the functionality

It is necessary to decide upon suitable functional groupings to be addressed by Timeboxes. Such groupings should make sense to the business representatives as well as the Solution Developers; grouping by function, business goal or user tasks is often appropriate. These functional groupings should be kept as small as possible to keep the Timeboxes short. Design considerations occasionally override business considerations. Some functionality will necessarily appear in more than one functional grouping. Such common functionality may be fundamental to the success of the increment and should be scheduled as early as possible. There will be some components which are acknowledged as important but which cannot be aligned to particular functions (for example, in a software project, building the database may fall into this category). These components must appear in the Development Timeboxes. When planning the Timebox schedule, the aim should be to identify all technical and architectural components that will be needed by the increment and to distribute them appropriately in the plan. Architectural components should be as clearly prioritised as the functions.

All the normal planning considerations must also apply, such as holidays. Overtime should not be built into the estimates; the plan should assume normal working hours.

3.3 The Iterative Development Process within the Development Timeboxes

At the Development Timebox level, it is essential to ensure that the process to be followed is disciplined enough to promote acceptable quality levels yet allow for creativity within the team.

Every Timebox can be viewed as comprising five main stages:

- *Kick-off :* This is usually a meeting of the Solution Development Team to confirm the objective(s), content, priorities and responsibilities within the Timebox and set review points and criteria (time required: about 1 to 3 hours per Timebox);

- *Investigation:* This involves the Solution Development Team's initial investigation of the detail of the products to be delivered in the Timebox, including agreement on what the Timebox is to deliver and quantitative measures (acceptance criteria) against which they will be measured by the end of the Timebox. These acceptance criteria are important to allow the team to know when they are 'done' with the work in the Timebox, and prevent the temptation to stop work just because the time has run out, thus delivering inadequate quality (time required: approximately 15% of Timebox);

- *Refinement:* This is where the bulk of the development and testing of the Timeboxes products, including documentation, will be done, in line with the already agreed priorities (time required: approximately 70% of Timebox);

- *Consolidation:* This is the final testing of products to ensure that all have met their acceptance criteria, completion of documentation and tying up of any loose ends to ensure that all work of the Timebox has been completed to the right quality level (time required: approximately 15% of Timebox);

- *Closeout:* This is a short meeting where the final formal acceptance of the Timebox products is agreed, particularly by the Business Visionary and Technical Co-ordinator. Any work scheduled but not completed within the Timebox should be recognised here and addressed, with appropriate action being decided upon. Any Must Have, Should Have or Could Have requirements which have not been covered will result in a level of replanning, which may affect other Development Timeboxes within the increment. If Must Haves are incomplete, the effect on the whole increment need to be assessed; if it is forecast that the project will not achieve at least the Must Haves, this must be drawn to the attention (i.e. escalated) of the next higher level of project governance. At the end of each Development Timebox, it is also worth running a short 'Retrospective Workshop' with the Solution Development Team and other relevant stakeholders, to gather feedback and lessons learned for the Timebox (time required: about 1 to 3 hours).

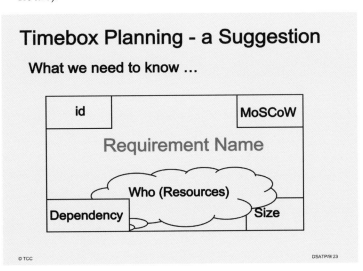

3.4 Daily Stand-up

Timebox progress should be considered on a daily basis at the short and a focused Daily Stand-up held throughout the Timebox. These are primarily a way for the team to understand progress and recognise risks and issues early.

3.5 Timeboxing and MoSCoW

In order to ensure that a Timebox will finish on time, there has to be a level of flexibility in the deliverables it must achieve. If there is no flexibility, estimates must be perfect and nothing unforeseen must delay progress (a situation which represents an impossible dream!). Thus, for the project as a whole, the requirements must be prioritised in terms of what is essential, and what could be managed without (at least for a while). The MoSCoW classification of requirements provides the basis for decisions about what the project team will do over the whole project, during any increment and during any Development Timebox within the project.

As new requirements arise or as existing requirements are defined in detail, the decision must be made as to how critical they are to the success of the current work, using the MoSCoW rules. All priorities should be reviewed throughout the project to ensure that they are still valid. It is the lower priority requirements that enable the teams to deliver on time, by de-scoping these if necessary when problems arise.

Timeboxes work through the effective application of empowerment. The team working in the Timebox must agree the objectives and make realistic estimates of the time required to achieve the Timebox objectives. At the Timebox Close Out meeting, the business representatives must be able to approve the delivery of the products covered by the Timebox. If it appears, at any point during the Timebox, that its deadline could be missed, the Solution Development Team is empowered to drop Should Have and Could Have requirements: the Timebox end should not slip! Continuous negotiation of what is important is at the Solution Development Team level. The Business Ambassadors in the team should have the casting vote on whether a requirement can be de-scoped, to keep the final product business focused. 'Slippage' and de-prioritisation of Must Haves usually necessitate escalation beyond the Solution Development Team.

3.6 Management of the Timebox

To achieve the benefits of Timeboxing, the following aspects need particular attention:

- *Planning:* Activities within the Timebox must be carefully and accurately planned (as far as possible) by the team, before the Timebox begins and during the Kick-off. There will be little time for planning activities subsequently;

- *Realistic objectives:* The amount to be achieved, from both the Solution Developer and Business Ambassador perspectives, must be clearly understood, and must be realistic within the time limit;

- *Realistic scope:* It is vital that the scope of the product is clearly defined and agreed by all parties before the work commences. Scope drift cannot be accommodated in a Timebox;

- *Effective management:* The manager of an Atern project must keep tight control over the use of time and resources. It will also be necessary to motivate all staff, and to communicate clearly the scope and objectives to all staff (and third parties, if appropriate), to ensure that the Timebox deadlines are visible to all involved parties and the need for contributions from different quarters does not result in delay;

- *Monitoring;* The progress of the project must be continuously monitored, for two purposes:

  - as work progresses, the Project Manager must ensure that the team continually identifies, and focuses on, the aspects of greatest relevance to the business;

  - any slippage must be identified immediately, during the Timebox, and the appropriate corrective action taken.

- *Clear definition of responsibilities:* It would be inappropriate to waste time by duplicating effort, or to discover at the end of the Timebox that key tasks had been overlooked. Clearly agreed terms of reference and Timebox responsibilities will help to prevent this;

- *Clear definition of deliverables:* The nature and content of the deliverables for each Development Timebox in the increment will be visible at Delivery Plan level at the end of Foundations. At Kick-off of each Development Timebox, the detail of the deliverables of the Timebox and clear acceptance criteria are established;

- *Commitment*: All individuals involved in the Timebox must be motivated and able to work on their own initiative to contribute to the objectives of the current Timebox and of the project as a whole;

- *Availability:* It is vital that the involvement of business representatives and other contributors is agreed early and is visibly included in the Delivery Plan and Timebox Plans. If the relevant people are not available at the relevant time, the completion of the Timebox or the quality of the product will be threatened.

3.7 Recommended approach to Development Timeboxes

At the project level, the Delivery Plan defines the Timeboxes within an increment. This ensures that the key business requirements (both functional and non-functional) are addressed in the most appropriate order, and that the availability of resources and ordering of Timeboxes matches those requirements.

Each Timebox should guarantee to deliver a clearly-defined product, to agreed acceptance criteria. Guaranteed deliverables can only be achieved if the Solution Development Teams agree that the estimated effort to deliver the Timebox product is well within their capability to achieve. As a rule of thumb, the following proportions of priorities in any Timebox are recommended:

- *Must Have* - approximately 60% of effort;

- *Should Have* - approximately 20% of effort;

- *Could Have* - approximately 20% of effort.

It is advised that the estimated effort in the Must Haves should never be above 75%. The only kind of project in which a higher level of Must Haves may be tolerable is one which is a fully-understood rewrite of an existing and already well-documented system. Even here, the risk of not delivering on time and within budget rises sharply with the proportion of Must Haves.

3.8 Planning the Development Timeboxes in the Delivery Plan

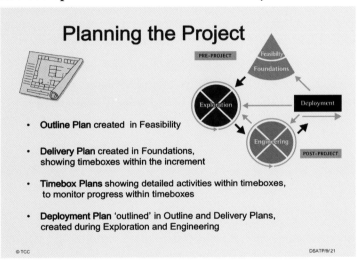

All of the information above comes together when we begin to place the functionality of the business (and technical) requirements into the Delivery Plan. The following steps are derived from using DSDM Atern in real life projects and may be useful:

- It is helpful, first of all, to give each requirement (i.e. each piece of work to be entered into the plan), a unique identifier, in order to cross-reference it for dependency and traceability;

- When creating a schedule of Development Timeboxes, the primary driver should always be the business priority;

- We have already had agreed priorities (MoSCoW) assigned to high level business requirements during Foundations. This must also be done for technical requirements. Where there is a hierarchy of dependent requirements, we must ensure consistency (e.g. a Must Have cannot be dependent on a prior Should Have);

- Dependencies between requirements should be analysed before planning the Development Timeboxes. Modelling techniques can be extremely helpful here, remembering to do EDUF – enough design up front, and no more! The risk here is one of delving into too much detail too early;

- The assignment of resources should be of specific (named) people, to allow the planner to ensure that any parallel tasks are feasible and that no-one is overloaded within any particular Development Timebox;

- The size of each requirement must be estimated, in terms of both business representative and Solution Developer effort (and that of any other persons involved), to avoid unrealistic planning and to allow the best use of each human resource. Estimates are in person-days or hours. However, elapsed time should also be considered, particularly where it will necessitate a requirement being completed over a number of Development Timeboxes. In such cases it is necessary to split the requirement into components, each of which can be completed within a Timebox. The use of 'Story Points' for estimating is a useful, best practice technique. This allows for comparative estimates to be made: a team member may say, "I don't know how long Requirement Y will take, but it will be about twice as long as Requirement X". Story Points would allow Requirement Y to be valued at twice the number of Story Points as Requirement X, without committing to actual hours or days. Initially, Story Points may be valued as being equal to hours. Then, if estimates are found to be over optimistic, the team can just re-value the Story Point in order to re-set similar estimates throughout the project!

The above guidance is not mandatory, but should assist in the production of a Delivery Plan which, if kept visible to the Solution Development Team throughout the project, will enable the project to be managed and controlled successfully.

4. Conclusion

This chapter has considered both estimating and Timeboxing, as essential elements of the planning of the DSDM Atern project.

Estimating involves forecasting the cost, effort, skills, person-hours and elapsed time to deliver a specific requirement or objective. Alternatively cost, effort, skills and time may be fixed, and the requirement is to forecast how much functionality can be delivered within these constraints.

A Timebox is a fixed period of time, at the end of which an objective has been met and a deliverable has been produced. Timeboxes are a powerful way of keeping a project under control, provided that the time deadline is not allowed to slip. In order to achieve this, the project stakeholders should agree that if time is threatened, the less-important features in any Timebox can be dropped.

By involving the right people in estimating, and by configuring Timeboxes with the right level of flexibility of Must Have, Should Have and Could Have requirements throughout the development, the DSDM Atern team will be able to monitor and control the project, adapt if the estimates are wrong and incorporate new requirements as the project progresses without having to take the project over time and over budget.

Estimating and Timeboxing

1. **The three levels of Timebox defined in DSDM Atern are:**

   A} Project; Increment; Development

   B} Iteration; Development; Programme

   C} Project; Monthly; Weekly

   D} Project; Stage; Work Package

2. **What is an increment?**

   A} A delivery of whatever is ready at the end of a Timebox

   B} A delivery of the Prioritised Requirements List

   C} A point on the salary scale related to a DSDM Atern project role

   D} A delivery of a complete and business-meaningful subset of the solution

3. **Timebox objectives are based on which DSDM Atern product?**

   A} Quality Plan

   B} Outline Plan

   C} Project Initiation Document

   D} Prioritised Requirements List

4. **What is the best mix of priorities in a Timebox?**

   A} Must = 20%, Should = 60%, Could = 10%, Won't = 10%

   B} Must = 60%, Should = 20%, Could = 20%, Won't = 0%

   C} Must = 25%, Should = 25%, Could = 25%, Won't = 25%

   D} Must = 80%, Should = 20%, Could = 0%, Won't = 0%

5. **What are the steps in a Development Timebox?**

   A} Kick Off, Creation, Refinement, Consolidation, Close Out

   b) Kick Off, Investigation, Refinement, Consolidation, Sign Off

   C} Plan, Investigation, Refinement, Consolidation, Sign Off

   D} Kick Off, Investigation, Refinement, Consolidation, Close Out

Answers can be found on page 222

Dynamic Systems Development Method

Estimating and Timeboxing

Session Objectives

- How do we estimate?

- The estimating process

- Estimating in the Atern lifecycle

- What is a Timebox?

- Planning the project

Atern 5 Key Techniques

- MoSCoW Prioritisation

- Modelling

- Facilitated Workshops

- Iterative Development

- Timeboxing

© TCC   DSATP/9/3

Estimating

Estimating Exercise

- *Build a wall*

Estimating

Estimating Exercise

- *Build a wall*

- *Make a journey*

© TCC

DSATP/9/6

Estimating

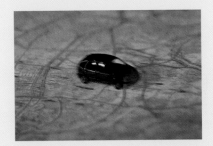

The Estimating Process

There are a number of distinct steps:

- Estimate the effort required

- Adjust the effort for environmental factors

- Identify the products and their inter-dependencies

- Schedule the product deliveries and allocate resource

- Adjust the schedule in the light of known constraints

Factors Affecting an Estimate

- Size of task

- Complexity

- Quality required

- Productivity of people

- Availability of resource

- Experience of people

© TCC

DSATP/9/9

Who Estimates?

The team estimates!

The Estimating Approaches

Approaches may be top-down or bottom up and include:

- Task based
- Product based
- Algorithmic
- Non-algorithmic
- Analogy
- Expert judgement
- Standard ratios
- Function point analysis

USE MORE THAN ONE APPROACH!

Why are Estimates Wrong?

- Inexperience of estimating

- Doing something that has not been done before

- Inadequate techniques

- Optimistic assumptions

- Wrong person making estimates

- Lack of information

© TCC   DSATP/9/ 12

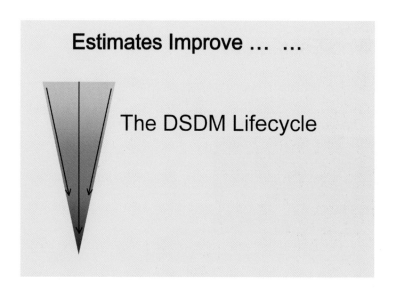

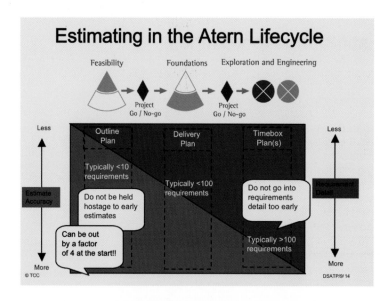

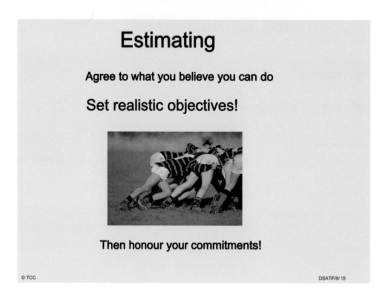

What is a Timebox?

> A timebox is a fixed period of time,
> at the end of which an objective has been met.

- The time available dictates work done

- The aim of a timebox is to make something useful!!

- A timebox is product-focused, not task-focused

The Mindset for Timeboxing

"Creative people in many walks of life have a deadline.
A magazine writer, television producer or seminar developer
creates material for a certain date.
James Martin

Whatever else happens,
they must not fail to meet the deadline."

© TCC
DSATP/9/17

The Delivery Plan

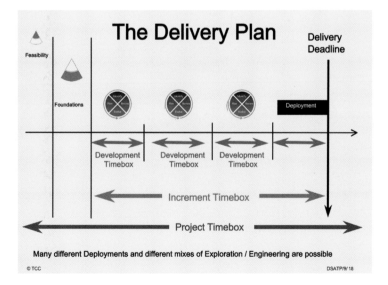

Many different Deployments and different mixes of Exploration / Engineering are possible

© TCC
DSATP/9/18

Size of a Development Timebox

How large should it be?

- 15 days?
- ~~6 days?~~
- ~~12 weeks?~~
- ~~6 weeks?~~

10 – 30 days
(2 - 6 weeks)

Timeboxing

As a rule of thumb, within timeboxes within an increment:

Must Have	approximately 60% of effort
Should Have	approximately 20% of effort
Could Have	approximately 20% of effort

The estimated effort in the Must Haves should never be above 75% (except in rewrites of well-documented systems)

Planning the Project

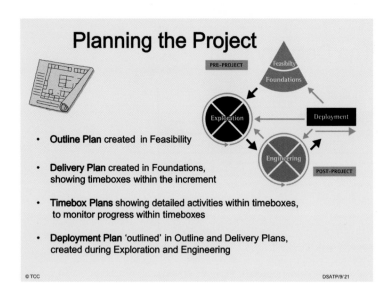

- **Outline Plan** created in Feasibility

- **Delivery Plan** created in Foundations, showing timeboxes within the increment

- **Timebox Plans** showing detailed activities within timeboxes, to monitor progress within timeboxes

- **Deployment Plan** 'outlined' in Outline and Delivery Plans, created during Exploration and Engineering

© TCC   DSATP/9/21

Timebox Plans

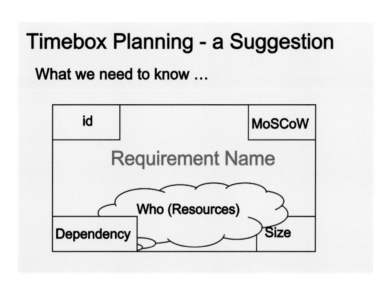

Timebox Planning - a Suggestion

What we need to know ...

id		MoSCoW
	Requirement Name	
	Who (Resources)	
Dependency		Size

Session Summary

- How do we estimate?

- The estimating process

- Estimating in the Atern lifecycle

- What is a Timebox?

- Planning the project

DSATP/9/24

Dynamic Systems Development Method

Estimating and Timeboxing

A Presentation and Negotiation Skills

PRESENTATION SKILLS

1. Introduction

There will always be a place for written communication both within and between business organisations and to customers but, more and more, the importance of actually talking to people is being recognised. It will come as no surprise then, that throughout our careers we may find ourselves in situations requiring a presentation.

Having been tasked, our emotions are likely to be mixed – a combination of worry, apprehension and excitement. We must always remember that our audience will judge us, our organisation, and often our product by the quality of our presentation.

To give a good quality presentation there is a need for us to do a lot of planning and preparing which is a time-consuming business. However, if we approach the task systematically, we will produce a presentation that will interest, entertain and persuade our audience. This thorough preparation will also go a long way towards helping us to overcome our nerves. We will have far less to worry about if we know that the content is right. This session gives guidelines to help you produce an effective presentation.

2. The Presentation Pyramid

In order to structure your preparation, think of it as a pyramid, which has to be built from the base upwards. The layers of the pyramid are:

- Plan;
- Prepare;
- Practice;
- Deliver.

Follow these as your preparation sequence for the presentation.

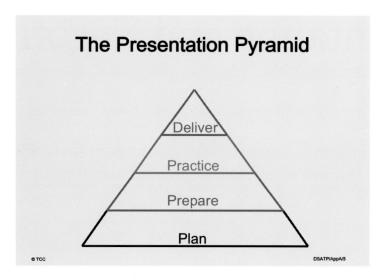

3. Plan

3.1 Know your audience

You are sitting at your desk with a blank sheet of paper in front of you. You have probably written the title of your presentation at the top of the page. The ideas start to flow. You scribble frantically. But what about the audience? Put them first, if you want to be persuasive and memorable.

Who are they?
- Customers?
- Board of Directors?
- Graduate trainees?
- Members of the golf club?
- Parent/teacher association?

How well do you know them?
- Close colleagues?
- Acquaintances?
- Total strangers?

How many of them are there?
- A small intimate group?
- A sea of faces?

Why are they coming to listen to you?
- Passive curiosity?
- Urgent need to know?
- Need to be convinced?
- They've been told to?

Level of knowledge
- What is their level of knowledge at the start of the presentation?
- Where do you want it to be at the end?

3.2 Identify the central message

Look back to the title of your presentation – for example, 'Introducing Flexible Working Time for all Administration Staff' – and think about how you might start off...

I'm here today to talk to you about introducing flexible working time for all administration staff.

Clear enough, but not very inviting or memorable. You've taken a lot of trouble to find out about your audience. Use that knowledge to find an aspect of your proposal that will appeal to them. Identify the purpose and benefit to them. Then create your central message – a single, pithy sentence which tells your audience why you're giving the presentation and what's in it for them.

If you're talking to the staff...

Flexitime means that while your neighbours are sweating through the rush hour, you can be walking the dog.

If you're talking to the Board...

With flexitime, you'll be open 11 hours a day with a crew of volunteers, and all it'll cost you is the electric light bill.

4. Prepare

4.1 Gather information

Despite all the work you've done so far, finding out about your audience and creating a central message, you now need to gather the information which will form the content of your presentation.

Don't start to write your presentation yet. It will be wasted effort! Instead of a breakdown have a brainstorm.

Work out the topics to be covered, and what is essential or just nice to have. Talk to an audience member. What do they want?

If you are familiar with mind-maps or spider diagrams, try drawing one of these. This enables you to see the extent of the subject, links best ideas, sparks new ideas and highlights the key points relevant to your central message and therefore of benefit to your audience.

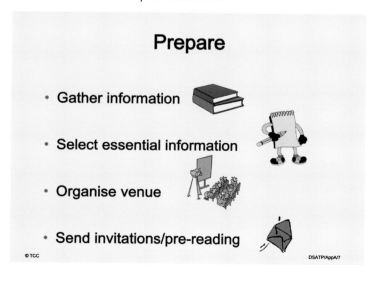

4.2 Select essential information

I could talk about it all night.

Does that ring a bell? Knowing a lot can present more problems than knowing a little. The most dangerous subject is the one that fascinates you, and that you're the world expert on – leave your anorak at home!!

Examine your own motives. Why are you including this point? Is it because your audience really wants or needs to know it, or is it just because you find it interesting?

Only choose points that really support your central message and make it more memorable.

Now put the information you've selected in two lists:

1. Vital to support your central message

2. Useful to reinforce it if there's time

Using this layout now will save you time later on if you need to alter or shorten your notes.

Whatever structure you choose, the most important thing is that you move logically from one section to the next and from one point to the next.

4.3 Organise venue

Book the venue and equipment for your presentation well in advance of your presentation, selecting a room of appropriate size for the expected number of attendees and the method of presentation.

4.4 Send invitations/pre-reading

People's time is in demand and to ensure that you have the right people at your presentation, send out invitations in good time. Background information should be issued where this will help clarify the issues and why individuals ought to be at the meeting.

4.5 Prepare your presentation

Sound preparation is the key to a good presentation of the information which you have selected to support your central message. A good structure forms the foundation.

Prepare the structure of the presentation

So you know what you want to say, but how are you going to structure it?

SITUATION   Explain the background and the present position – yours and theirs.

NEED   Show the audience that you have a good understanding of their needs; that you are aware of their problems.

ALTERNATIVES   Outline the options that the audience has to improve the situation. Remember your solution isn't necessarily the only one.

PROPOSAL   Make your own case, linking it to the central message, to show how your audience will benefit.

**Prepare
Structure of Presentation**

- P resent position
- P roblems we face
- P ossibilities
- P roposal

© TCC   DSATP/AppA/10

Prepare the body of the presentation

This element of your presentation is where you build your central message for your audience. Unfortunately it is also the longest section and therefore the most likely period for your audience to flag unless you take steps to hold their attention.

It is not unusual during a presentation for an audience to lose concentration. The pattern will be the same no matter how long or short your overall presentation is. You are not going to get your message across if the audience isn't awake, attentive and active throughout. So you need to turn the attention troughs into peaks by making everything as clear and memorable as possible – the structure you've chosen, the talk time in minutes, the language you use, and the information you're presenting.

Look again at your structure. Break it down into sections to create more beginnings and endings since these are the periods when the audience's attention is at its best.

Now think about how to keep them with you when you move from section to section.

Prepare
Introduction

- Who are you?
- What qualification?
- SNAP
- Length and format
- When questions taken

© TCC   DSATP/AppA/13

Prepare the introduction
"Good morning ladies and gentlemen..."

By now you've a pretty good idea of:

- What you want to cover;
- How you're going to cover it;
- How long it's going to take.

But how are you going to introduce yourself and the subject of your presentation?

It is useful to have a route map for your introduction:

- Welcome;
- Who I am;
- What 'qualifies' me to speak;
- A synopsis of SNAP;
- How long it will take and the format;
- When I will be happy to take questions.

You should never include anything in your introduction that you will not include in the main body of your presentation.

Prepare
Conclusion

- Finish on time
- Summarise (nothing new)
- What action now required
- Questions

© TCC   DSATP/AppA/14

Prepare the conclusion
So, Ladies and Gentlemen, just to sum up...

By now, you should have the audience's full attention. This is the last chance to drive home your central message.

Don't add any new information at this stage: it'll only confuse. Just briefly restate your main points or proposal – using different words to avoid sounding repetitive. And try to finish on a high note.

Try and anticipate some of the questions you may get by thinking from the audience viewpoint, particularly if the group is made up of people from different job functions, e.g. a Marketing Manager has a different viewpoint from that of a Finance Director. But don't attempt to answer all possible questions in your presentation. Get your messages across according to your objective and in the right time.

4.6 It's not just what you say, it's how you say it!!

You've produced your plan; you've got a structure with a clear, punchy introduction, and a pithy conclusion. Is that enough to make sure you push the point home?

Signposting
A writer can show his reader that he's switching subjects, returning to an earlier theme, or concluding. He uses paragraphs. Presenters can't.

At every stage, tell your audience where they are, where they've been, and where they're going. Remember, your aim is to help them grasp your ideas easily, not battle with your logic.

Use signposts to:

Start a section	*OK. Let's start by...*
Change sections	*Perhaps we could move on to the question of...*
Reinforce the central message	*What does that mean to you?*
Look ahead	*I'll come back to this point later*
Look back	*As I mentioned earlier...*
Link	*...and that ties with...*
Summarise	*So, what does it boil down to?*
Conclude	*I think that covers everything*

Use signposts too, to establish an understanding between you and your audience.

Show them that you:

Understand their needs	*and this, of course, is why you want to...*
Sympathise with their views	*You're absolutely right when you say...*

Anticipate their questions	*You're probably wondering why we...*
Appreciate their expertise	*I don't need to tell you that...*

Use of language and painting pictures with words

Using concrete words, short sentences and word pictures usually works well and is particularly effective for emphasis of key points. This technique can help to get your message across to your audience in a clear, punchy and concise way. But don't overdo it – use it as a variant for grabbing audience attention.

When you think of your favourite film, what springs first to mind? The actual words the actors used, or a visual impression of what went on? The visual memory is very powerful. Use it.

Paint word pictures – as wide a range as possible – with similes and visual analogies:

The control unit handles all interconnections in the system. Think of it as a telephone exchange serving a town.

See how far you can extend it, without labouring the point (switchboards, party lines, engaged signals, phone numbers, bills):

If you want to send a message to another terminal, that's just like ringing a friend in the same town.

Invite them to visualise the scene:

And there's Doris. You can hardly see her behind the mountain of paper in her in-tray. And she's trying to decide which of the four phones to answer first!

Put your points into a list of three, building up to a climax:

1 So, you're all aware there's a gap.

2 You know the gap has to be filled.

3 We have the way to fill it.

The rhythm of **3** works for individual words too:

It's going to be difficult, no question.

But in the end it'll be efficient (1), modern (2) and,

above all, profitable (3).

Enhance the effect by using words with the same initial letter and sound:

*It's going to be **Painful**, no question.*

*But in the end it'll be **Productive**,*

***Progressive** and, above all, **Profitable**.*

If you want the audience to reject an alternative, build up a case for it, then knock it down with one or two sentences:

Sure it's cheap,

Available from stock.

Installation is no problem.

User friendly too.

But...

It's totally incompatible with any other system.

Take it, and you've lost all your flexibility.

Prepare Visual Aids

- Flipchart
- OHP and transparencies
- Desktop projector
- LCD panel
- 35mm slides
- Other?

© TCC   DSATP/AppA/15

Prepare visual aids NOT liabilities

We've talked about making the structure clear and the language visual, but what about using visual aids themselves?

The range is wide. From real objects and samples, wall charts and pin boards, to slides, computer graphics and video tape. What resources do you have at your disposal to produce and show them?

Perhaps you're having your visual aids created and produced for you by experts, or perhaps you're putting them together yourself. There may be just an overhead projector in the presentation room, or a sophisticated computer and video system.

However simple or sophisticated your visual aids are, when should you use them? What should they look like? How should you show them?

Check each visual for size, colour, content and variety.

Will the audience be able to see and understand it from the back? It's especially important to check if you're producing visuals from the printed page.

Experiment with different colour combinations and look at the results with a fresh eye. Which point do you want to highlight? Does it stand out better in red or black? What happens if you change the background colour?

Stick to one idea per visual and keep it uncluttered. Use it to throw light on an otherwise complex point.

You don't want all the visuals to look the same. Make them as varied as possible.

5. Practice

· ·

If you are well-prepared it will be self evident and you will take your audience logically through your presentation. A good way of preparing yourself is to...

REHEARSE

REHEARSE

REHEARSE:

- On your own – OUT LOUD;

- In front of a mirror;

- To a colleague(s);

- To a family member(s).

Build rehearsal time into your preparation!

5.1 Voice and language

Think about your voice and the language you use:

- Speed – not too fast or slow;

- Strength of voice – speaking too loudly is not a problem but mumbling, garbling and whispering is;

- Pitch – this can give emphasis to key points;

- Pace – change the pace;

- Pause – to allow assimilation of ideas;

- Keep it simple – avoid jargon;

- Use (the right sort of) humour;

- Smile;

- Explain the whole before the parts.

Remember, variety will hold your audience's attention.

Check the timing.

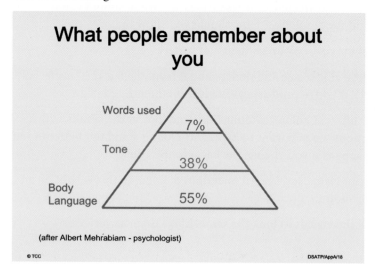

5.2 Checking body language

Again, a colleague might be able to help you here.

Any mannerisms that you have (head scratching, pacing up and down, fiddling about in your pocket, waving your hands around) are fine unless the audience finds them more interesting than what you're saying.

Throat clearing, 'ah's and 'hm's between sentences, verbal tics (you know? OK? yeah? sort of, right?) can distract or irritate if they're too frequent.

6. Deliver

6.1 Making the final checks – pre-delivery

Have you got your notes in order?

Are they legible?

Have you checked your timing?

Are you sure you're not going to speak for too long?

Are you using visuals? If so, are they in order?

What about the equipment? Have you tried it out? Is it in the right position? Can you use it without fumbling?

Have you checked the room?

Where will you be standing or sitting?

Will they be able to hear you and see you from the back? Have you got a microphone?

Is the lighting OK?

Is everything else you might need – paper, pens, pointers – to hand?

Have you got enough copies of any hand-outs you're giving them at the end?

Final checks

1. Notes in order?
2. Timing OK?
3. Visual aids in order
4. Equipment checked?
5. Room checked?
6. Sufficient hand-outs?
7. Is the reason for the presentation still valid?

© TCC   DSATP/AppA/1

6.2 Using your visuals

When it comes to showing the visuals within your presentation there are a number of tips which help to make their use effective:

• Be sensitive. Either you prepared your own visual, or you know it extremely well, but your audience hasn't seen it before;

- *Position* yourself so that everyone can see. You don't want the Managing Director craning his neck or squinting. If you're right handed, stand with the visual on *your* right;

- *Signpost* each visual briefly before you show it to them;

- Stay quiet while they absorb it before you start talking. A simple graph with two axes, one curve and a title takes at least 7 seconds to absorb and understand; and that's assuming the audience are used to such visuals;

- Then make your point and explain. Keep your eyes on the audience and talk to them, not the visual – even if their eyes are not on you;

- Switch off the machine or take the visual away when you've finished with it.

Remember, you need about two minutes per visual: to put it up, to give the audience time to absorb it, then to explain it and draw conclusions from it. So, make sure you haven't got too many. Strike a balance between visual aids and apt analogies.

6.3 Eye contact

Make an effort not to look at the ceiling or floor. The audience will sense your confidence has gone.

Remember to look at the audiences and not your visual aid.

Look around and establish eye contact, even with the people who are sitting at the sides of the room. If you focus on the person in front of you, you'll make him feel guilty and the others will switch off.

6.4 Handling questions

Assessing how your message is being received can be done in two major ways. Looking at the physical reaction of the group i.e. their body language, and seeing what questions are asked.

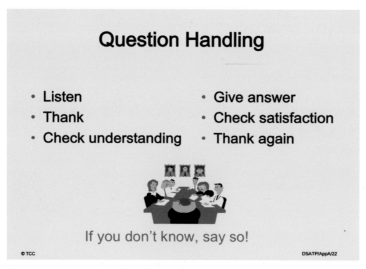

If you are interrupted with a question you don't want to answer at that time, explain why and when you will answer it. Note the question down and remember to answer it at the right time. Refer specifically to the question to show them that this is their answer.

Questions are a positive sign of interest and allow us to check the groups understanding. When handling questions from the floor, follow this procedure:

- Listen carefully to the question and note it down if necessary;

- Thank the questioner;

- Check that you understand it – if necessary ask for more information or re-phrase or translate it;

- Give your answer – be brief, think first of your answer so that you are concise;

- Check you have answered fully;

- Thank them again

A question session at the end shows you have stimulated the group to think seriously about your presentation.

7. Summary of Presentation Skills

Remember:

- Plan;

- Prepare;

- Practice;

- Deliver.

But especially remember:

FAILURE TO PREPARE IS PREPARATION TO FAIL

NEGOTIATION

8. Negotiation is About People

Negotiation is a process in which ego and emotions can easily become involved but we should be conscious of the impact of such emotion on our negotiating ability. *Always keep in mind the objective issues that are involved.* When we allow emotions to get carried away with us the entire process is undermined or real issues are sacrificed in order to satisfy emotional needs. Carried too far, the desire to be the winner in a negotiation will necessarily mean that the other party is a loser.

Negotiation is about developing and managing relationships during the negotiation. It is possible to be hard-nosed and tough, and still establish a good relationship with high levels of credibility. The key is to separate the conflict elements, which are business-driven, from positive personal elements, which relate to you and the other party as people.

Don't forget that the negotiating process can, for many people, be one of the most stressful aspects of a relationship. What occurs during the negotiating process may well have a major impact on the long-term relationship that you are establishing.

9. The Four Stages of Negotiation

There are four stages to any negotiation each of them critical to a successful (for both parties) outcome of the negotiation process. These are:

- Prepare;
- Discuss;
- Propose;
- Bargain.

9.1 Prepare

Negotiation planning is never wasted

Occasionally we get a nice surprise. We plan extensively for a negotiation, only to find that the other party agrees with all or most of our position. Wonderful! Close the deal and move on to the next. You didn't waste your time planning. If there had been major opposition, you would have been ready.

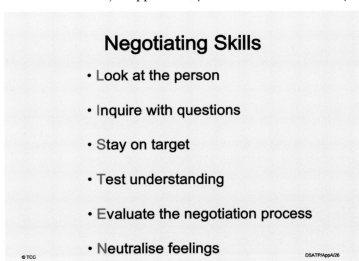

A few common sense rules will help prepare for the negotiation by reducing conflict, turning it into cooperation to allow solutions that really work for all the participants to be reached.

- *Separate the people from the problem:* If we view the problem as that which needs to be resolved, rather than viewing someone as holding a contrary viewpoint or as a person to be defeated, the odds of a successful negotiation increase. One simple idea, executed in preparing the venue for the negotiation, is to change the shape of the table; rather than sitting opposite your 'opponents', arrange the seating so that all the parties are sitting together facing a flip chart or whiteboard, where the problem is presented. The covert message is that all the participants are facing the problem together – instead of it being 'us' against 'them', it is a case of 'all of us' against 'it';

- *Distinguish between interests and positions*: Consider the story of two sisters fighting over the only orange in the fruit bowl. Each sister must have the entire orange for herself – apparently any less is impossible. A wise negotiator asks each of the girls (in private) why she wants the orange. One explains she wants to drink the juice; the other wants to use the rind to cook a pudding. What each sister wants is her position, why she wants it is her interest. In this case, the simple solution is to give the cook the rind after the juice has been squeezed for the thirsty sister – thus meeting the interests of both is possible although their initial position was one of conflict;

- *When preparing* for a negotiation don't just ask "What do they want?" It is also important to ask, "Why do they want it?" It is equally important, and often more difficult to ask the same questions of yourself. Many successful negotiators find they will be more successful if they focus on understanding their interests as they enter discussions. If they start out with an open mind, the ideas of others may actually improve their final result;

- *Prepare your objectives:* What you wish to achieve and alternative ways of achieving them. Decide which objectives are fixed and which have some flexibility within which you can negotiate;

- *Plan the negotiation sequence:* Raise less contentious issues first and try to anticipate the likely response of the other party to your issues;

- *Do not prepare a complete package:* Negotiators who arrive with a complete package can create real problems. Modifications to their ideas might be taken personally, they may be stubborn, and reaching a satisfactory resolution is made more difficult.

9.2 Discuss

Once the negotiation process has entered the discussion phase, both parties are trying to gather information about the other's position whilst sitting at the negotiating table. By understanding the other party's position and interests you are equipping yourself with what needs to be achieved to satisfy the other party's needs, not that all of them may be satisfied of course!!

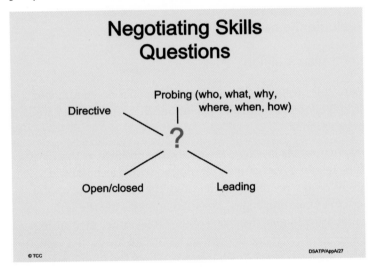

Questioning can be open or closed, or leading but should certainly seek to probe and elicit relevant information.

During this and subsequent phases people are signalling and it is very important to watch for these signals as the negotiation proceeds. Sometimes signals are overt and quite clear, but often they are subtle and easy to miss. But these signals can be of three types:

- Signals that people intend to send and that are true. Instead of saying things outright the information is given while preserving some degree of deniability – *"I didn't actually say that"*;

- Second, there are signals that people intend to send that are false. These signals are calculated to mislead you and direct you away from the other party's true goals;

- Third, the unintentional signal that slips out can provide critical information on what they want or will accept. These unintended signals can be very valuable, provided that you can distinguish them from the misleading ones!!

Sometimes a negotiator can act or appear to be irrational, use anger and intimidation, use jargon, and so forth to throw the other negotiating party and compromise their ability to negotiate effectively. Occasionally you will encounter a situation where an individual is truly upset or angry. In such a case it is important to deal with the emotional aspects before trying to continue with the process.

Active listening is a crucial tool in the negotiation process. If you do not actively listen how can you get a clearer picture of the other party's ideas. And when the listener's response shows just how good a job he or she has done listening, it can shock the other party:

"Good grief, they actually paid attention to me!"

Active listening forces a disciplined approach to focus on other opinions, giving the listener the chance to reflect on the process and strategy. The discipline of active listening requires that you focus on what another person is saying; don't spend your time shaping a stinging response that will put them in their place. Stepping aside and taking a dispassionate view of the goings-on can make one a far more effective negotiator.

Implied in active listening is that the listener has to be silent. You can't talk and listen at the same time and therefore understand the other party's opinion. In turn you won't be able to make an intelligent response to an opinion you do not understand.

Silence can be as effective a tool as speech. If one party is highly opinionated or emotional, if their approach is threatening or extremely demanding, keeping quiet after they finish speaking can be quite unsettling to them. Most people are troubled by silence in the midst of heated discussion. Sometimes silence is viewed as disapproval – but since no specific disapproval has been voiced, it cannot be treated as an attack. It has happened on many occasions that, when met with silence, people have modified their previous statements to make them more palatable!!

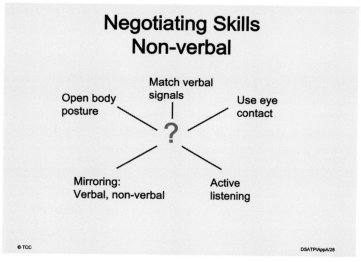

It takes at least two to argue!! To help individuals keep a cool head and pay attention to the process and the strategy, as well as the substance of the negotiation, only one person should be allowed to become angry at any one time, although it is preferable that no one gets to this emotional state. Yelling at each other is not negotiation; it is confrontation. In those situations there may possibly be a 'winner'; but it is even more likely there will be a 'loser'. If it's not your 'turn' to be angry, the exercise of restraint can be turned into a positive opportunity to observe what is going on with a clear eye.

9.3 Propose

Each party may make proposal and counter-proposal during the negotiation process with each of these becoming the boundaries between which compromise and negotiation can be enacted.

Sometimes a deadlock can occur – in fact negotiation may be considered to be a process of managing a series of short-term deadlocks. We declare a negotiation 'deadlocked,' and that may appear to be an end to it. It appears that there is no reasonable expectation for enough further movement on either side to bridge the remaining gap between the parties. If, however, you determine that you still wish to see the negotiation continue, there are a number of steps that you can take to accomplish this:

- Move the discussion away from the deadlock zone by changing issues;
- Try to find agreements in principle;
- Adjourn but do not end the negotiating session;
- Bring in other parties;
- Develop new information;
- Move to a more informal setting.

Any means to take any heat, disappointment, exhaustion, frustration and so on out of the process can bring renewed determination and vigour to the negotiation and allow a bargain to be achieved.

9.4 Bargain

Bargaining can only be successful if all participants perceive the process as fair. Participants are more likely to take it seriously and 'buy into' its result if this is the case. Moreover, the focus on fairness can have an important impact on the substantive result.

The notion before or even after a negotiation that *"we really stuffed them"* embodies a recognised sense of calculated unfairness that will leave the *"stuffed"* party aggrieved in the very least. To be considered successful, an agreement must be durable and parties who walk away from the table grumbling may regret their commitment and only honour it grudgingly. If they end up looking for excuses to get out from under an unwanted result, the gains achieved by the other side may prove to be short-term indeed.

In bargaining, the phrase of the format "If we provide…, then perhaps you could do… for us" is a useful tool to bring parties closer to agreement. Try to concede things that are 'cheap' for you to give but 'worth a lot' to the other party.

It is very common in the negotiating process for the agreement to come together at the last minute. To the outside observer it may appear as though nothing is happening, and then all at once, at the 11th hour, an agreement materializes. This occurs in part because of the need for an early feeling-out process during which time no agreements are reached and in part because each side is waiting for the other side to make concessions first. Neither side sees a reason to concede until time pressures force them to do so at the last minute.

Another pattern that is quite common is for the parties to reach agreement on some of the easier issues early on in the process, while the remaining difficult issues are resolved at the last minute.

Be aware of these patterns, be patient, and don't assume that because you are reaching the end of the time available that there will be a deadlock.

The ideal outcome from a negotiation meeting is the scenario where both parties feel that they have won: the 'WIN-WIN' outcome. Each party may not have won everything that they had wished for but success is achieved through a series of discussion, proposal and bargaining phases which explore the flexibilities in each party's interests.

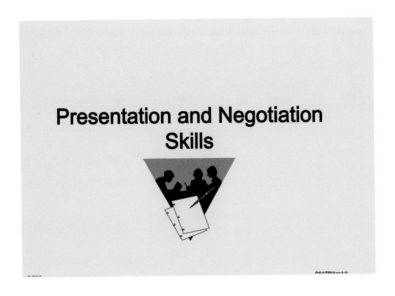

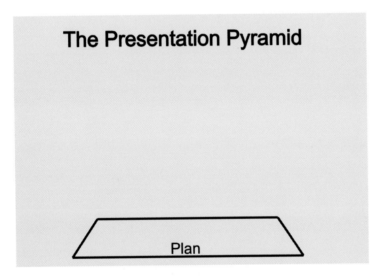

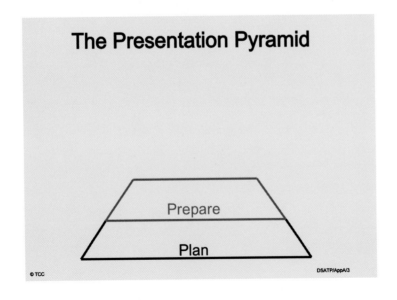

The Presentation Pyramid

The Presentation Pyramid

Plan

- Know your audience

Where do they start?
Where should they be at end?

- **Identify central message**

Purpose + benefit

© TCC   DSATP/AppA/6

Prepare

- Gather information

- Select essential information

- Organise venue

- Send invitations/pre-reading

© TCC   DSATP/AppA/7

Prepare
Order of Preparation

- Body

- Introduction

- Conclusion

Prepare
Structure of Presentation

- **S** ituation

- **N** eed

- **A** lternatives

- **P** roposal

© TCC   DSATP/AppA/9

Prepare
Structure of Presentation

- **P** resent position

- **P** roblems we face

- **P** ossibilities

- **P** roposal

DSATP/AppA/10

Prepare
Body

- Audience concentration level

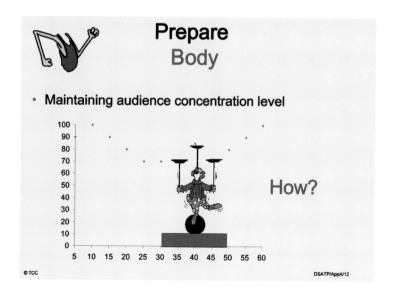

Prepare
Body

- Maintaining audience concentration level

How?

© TCC

DSATP/AppA/12

Prepare
Introduction

- Who are you?
- What qualification?
- SNAP
- Length and format
- When questions taken

Prepare
Conclusion

- Finish on time
- Summarise (nothing new)
- What action now required
- Questions

Prepare
Visual Aids

- Flipchart
- OHP and transparencies
- Desktop projector
- LCD panel
- 35mm slides
- Other?

© TCC

DSATP/AppA/15

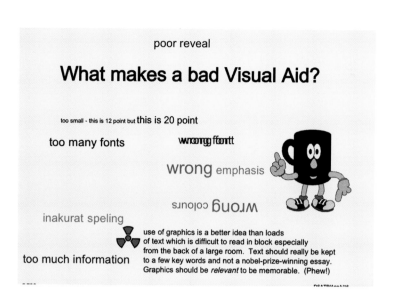

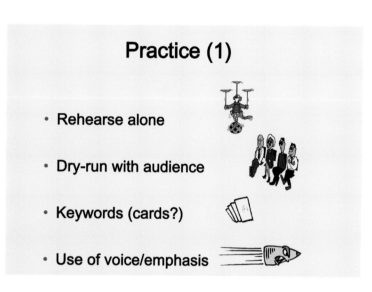

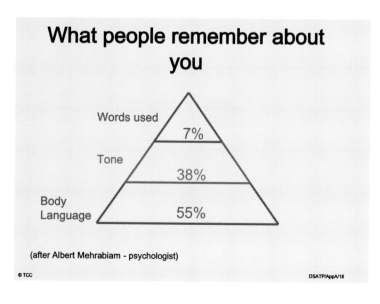

Practice (2)

- Body language

- Appearance

- Anticipate questions

- Timing

Final checks

1. Notes in order?
2. Timing OK?
3. Visual aids in order
4. Equipment checked?
5. Room checked?
6. Sufficient hand-outs?
7. Is the reason for the presentation still valid?

Deliver
Order of Presentation

- Introduction

- Body

- Conclusion

© TCC

DSATP/AppA/21

Question Handling

- Listen
- Thank
- Check understanding
- Give answer
- Check satisfaction
- Thank again

If you don't know, say so!

Presentation Skills Summary

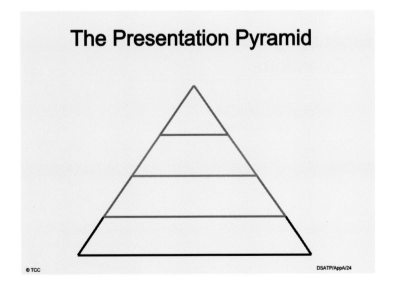

Remember: Failure to prepare is preparing to fail!

© TCC   DSATP/AppA/23

The Presentation Pyramid

© TCC   DSATP/AppA/24

Negotiation

- Prepare

- Discuss

- Propose

- Bargain

Negotiating Skills

- Look at the person

- Inquire with questions

- Stay on target

- Test understanding

- Evaluate the negotiation process

- Neutralise feelings

© TCC

DSATP/AppA/26

Negotiating Skills
Questions

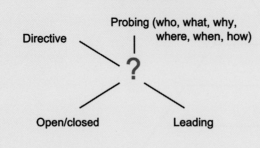

Directive

Probing (who, what, why, where, when, how)

?

Open/closed

Leading

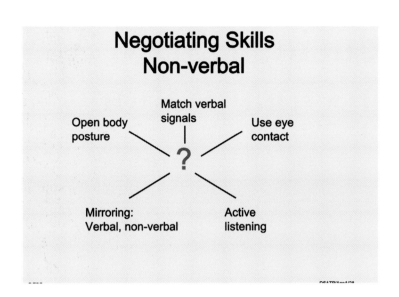

Introducing DSDM Atern into an Organisation

A Plan of Action

The introduction of DSDM Atern into an organisation must be carefully planned and managed to achieve a successful outcome.

Firstly, the reasons for introducing DSDM Atern must be understood. External pressures on the business may force the issue, such as market pressure or legislative changes. In these cases the business will be keen to apply DSDM Atern to meet their needs, and will bring pressure to bear on their IT departments. In other situations, IT departments themselves initiate the move towards DSDM Atern, often because of the need to gain greater commitment and involvement from the business, in order to deliver the right systems.

In any situation, the business case for DSDM Atern will need to be developed. It must show that there is a strong enough case for changing from the current approach to DSDM Atern. It should be put together in close collaboration between the business and IT departments.

Once the case for introducing DSDM Atern is established, it will be necessary to put together a plan for its implementation. This plan would typically be as follows:

1. **Identify a DSDM Atern champion**

   The successful implementation of DSDM Atern has often been driven by one individual who strongly believes in DSDM Atern and is driven to challenge and change the existing organisation's culture and current practices wherever relevant. These champions will be invaluable in convincing the sceptics, especially when they come from senior positions in the business.

2. **Communicate the philosophy and concepts of DSDM Atern to all concerned**

   This is normally achieved by a series of DSDM Atern awareness training courses, usually targeted at senior management and board level directors (both business and IT), all affected categories of business users, and IT development and support staff. In larger organisations, these events are run for the group of people identified to be involved on the first DSDM Atern project and planned implementation.

3. **Examine the current development practices and procedures, and compare with the DSDM Atern approach**

> For many organisations, they find that they have already been using elements of DSDM Atern, such as user involvement, empowerment, prototyping, facilitated workshops and Timeboxing. By using examples of successful practices already in use, adopting DSDM Atern can be seen to be building on existing best practice.

4. **Identify the areas that will need to be changed**

> In organisations where there is a large gap between the current culture and that required for DSDM Atern, a full change management programme should be put together. This may require the use of specialist, external consultants. Even if the gap is relatively small, it is still necessary to put together a plan. Some typical issues that need addressing are empowerment, multi-skilled team members and technical skills. The use of the MoSCoW rules can help to prioritise the plan.

> Where there are gaps in existing practices and procedures, the method of filling the gap must be identified, either for immediate action or during a pilot project which can feed its experiences back into the organisation's procedures. The latter approach should only be used for relatively minor changes to, or deficiencies in, current methods of working.

5. **Gain support and commitment for all the activities in the plan**

> Once support is gained for the plan, it will be possible to carry out all the necessary preparatory work in order to have a sound basis for starting on the first project.

6. **Identify the first project**

> Use the DSDM Atern Project Approach Questionnaire (PAQ) and Instrumental Success Factors (ISFs) to identify a suitable project. Some organisations will select projects to address urgent business needs, where there is no alternative but DSDM Atern to meet the tight deadline. Others will select a project for a business area, where they have already established good, close, working relationships with senior business management and key users. In all cases, assess the risks and agree how these will be managed.

> A key concern will be selecting suitable team members, using the DSDM Atern role definitions for guidance.

7. **Train the project team**

> All members of the team, both full and part time, should be trained using appropriate and accredited DSDM Atern training courses. It may also be necessary to provide technical training for tools, Configuration Management, testing etc.

8. **Set up the development environment**

> It is best to locate the DSDM Atern team in a dedicated room, in the business department. This room should contain all the technical equipment required for the team.

9. **Launch the project**

> Once everything is prepared, there will typically be some type of project launch event. This may take the form of a presentation of the business vision by the Visionary, team building events, a social occasion, an open day or a combination of such events.

10. **Run the first project**

> Often, an organisation will commission a DSDM Atern Coach to assist on the first project, to ensure that the DSDM Atern approach is being followed correctly, and that the team maintain their focus on delivering business benefits throughout the project. Indeed a DSDM Atern Mentor can be very useful before the project starts in helping to identify what changes to existing working practices should be considered.

11. **Review the project**

> Following the successful implementation of the first project, it is recommended that some time is spent analysing the project, particularly to identify lessons learnt. What will be done differently the next time? What will be kept the same? Particular attention should be paid to documents, procedures and any conflicts with existing work practices. These results should be documented and fed back into the next project.

12. **Broadcast your success**

> It is useful to put together presentations, videos, newsletters, press articles, etc. to let everyone in the organisation know of the success. This often leads to other departments then asking for DSDM Atern projects.

13. **Apply for DSDM Atern Practitioner certification**

> Members of the team may wish to apply for DSDM Atern Practitioner certification, thus gaining a professional qualification in DSDM Atern. Examination guidelines are available from the DSDM Atern Consortium.

14. **Prepare for the next DSDM Atern projects**

> In the early stages of propagating DSDM Atern in an organisation, many companies divide the existing DSDM Atern team members into two new teams and supplement them with inexperienced DSDM Atern team members. This is seen as a way to grow more teams, whilst retaining some experienced DSDM Atern developers in each team. Other organisations find splitting up successful teams too disruptive and keep successful teams together for as long as possible.

15. **Finally, measure the business benefits**

> Were the anticipated benefits achieved? Has the business case put forward been substantiated? It is wise to consider both hard and soft benefits – one of the typical benefits of the first DSDM Atern project is the clearer understanding in both business and IT of each other's different points of view. For some companies, this has considerably improved the relationship between business and IT departments.

C   DSDM Atern Glossary

TERM	EXPLANATION
80:20 rule	A rule of thumb stating that 80% of consequences stem from 20% of causes. For example, 80% of benefits stem from 20% of features. Also known as the Pareto Principle, it advocates pragmatism on a DSDM Atern project.
Baseline	A snapshot of a product, recorded and preserved at a point in time, as a known status to return to, if necessary.
Best practice	The concept of sharing experiences with other people or organisations in order to come up with ideas and practices that represent the best way to approach a problem or opportunity.
Bottom-up Estimating	Estimating each component individually and adding the estimates to achieve an overall estimate.
Burn-down Chart	A cumulative graph showing a descending trend of completed features against time within a Timebox.
Burn-up Chart	A cumulative graph showing an ascending graph of completed features, or earned value, within a Timebox.
Business Area Definition (BAD)	An element of the Business Foundations Product produced during the Foundations phase.
Cheese	A colloquialism for the Feasibility and Foundations phases, which are represented on the DSDM Atern lifecycle diagram as a cheese shape.

CM/Configuration Management	The discipline of managing the state of a product or set of related products.
Deliverable	A product. Something produced during the project.
Deployment	A lifecycle phase that focuses on getting the solution or part of it into operational use.
Development Timebox	The lowest level of Timebox. It is this Timebox that would be divided into cycles of investigation, refinement and consolidation.
Domain	A perspective or viewpoint of a project. There are three: Business, Solutions and Management.
DSDM/DSDM Consortium	The DSDM Consortium is the guardian of the DSDM Atern framework. DSDM stands for Dynamic Systems Development Method.
EDUF	This stands for Enough Design Up-Front. This is in contrast to Big Design Up-Front (BDUF) and No Design Up-Front (No DUF). BDUF and NoDUF are not recommended by DSDM.
Engineering	A lifecycle phase used iteratively and incrementally to evolve the solution created during Exploration to operational readiness.
Exploration	A lifecycle phase used iteratively and incrementally to investigate the requirements in detail and translate them into a form which can then be evolved into a viable solution.
Facilitated Workshop	A Facilitated Workshop is a gathering together of a group of people with the right skills and empowerment to produce a required product. It is co-ordinated by an impartial Facilitator, who enables the group to work collaboratively to achieve a predetermined objective.
Facilitator	An independent role in a Workshop, responsible for the Workshop process and managing the group dynamics.
Feasibility	A lifecycle phase that gives the first opportunity for deciding whether or not the project is viable from a technical and business perspective.

Foundations	A lifecycle phase to establish a firm basis for the rest of the project, from the three perspectives (domains) of Business, Solutions and Management.
Framework	A collection of principles, processes, roles and practices that provide a way to run projects. Framework is a similar term to 'method' and 'approach'.
Function/Feature	See Requirement.
Functional Requirement	A definition of an aspect of WHAT the product of the project needs to do to satisfy business need and the project objective. A feature or function. A User Story.
Increment	A partial delivery of the final product, preferably into operational use if possible. The term can also be used to describe a part of the project which creates a delivery of product.
Issue	Any concern, query or event that has happened, or is happening, that affects the project.
Iteration	A general term for working in a cyclic way. One pass of the Identify, Plan, Evolve, Review cycle in a Development Timebox.
Iterative Development	A DSDM Atern technique that allows evolution of a solution by prototyping and successive passes through investigation, refinement and consolidation. It allows validation of the understanding of the business needs and verification that the solution is being built correctly. It is used as a technique for communication and prototyping to converge on an accurate solution.
Lifecycle	A series of phases that a project goes through. The DSDM Atern Lifecycle has seven phases.
Minimum Usable Subset	The minimum amount of a project that needs to be delivered in order to provide a workable solution. The Must Haves.
Model	A representation of some or all of a product, produced in order to aid understanding or facilitate testing. It is usually a diagram, a picture or a prototype.

MoSCoW	A prioritisation technique used on requirements and tests, where M stands for Must Have, S stands for Should Have, C stands for Could Have and W stands for Won't Have this time.
Non-functional Requirement	A performance attribute. This can relate to the products of a project, a requirement, or a group of requirements. It specifies 'how well' or 'to what level' the product needs to perform. Examples of non-functional requirements are: performance, response time, security, availability, reliability.
PAQ (Project Approach Questionnaire)	A series of questions designed to establish a favourable environment for the conduct of a DSDM Atern project, where the eight principles can be adhered to and risks to project success are minimised.
Phase	A part of the DSDM Atern lifecycle. There are seven phases in the DSDM Atern lifecycle.
Pizza	A colloquialism for either the Exploration phase or the Engineering phase of a project, which are shown as circles on the DSDM Atern lifecycle diagram.
Post-Project	The DSDM Atern lifecycle phase which takes place after the last Deployment, where benefits realisation is assessed.
Pre-Project	The DSDM Atern lifecycle phase where the initial idea or imperative for a project is formalised in order for a project to be initiated.
Principle	A 'natural law' which acts as an attitude to take, and a mindset to adopt, on a DSDM Atern project.
Prioritised Requirements List (PRL)	A list of requirements for the project, which have been prioritised using the MoSCoW technique.
Product	The name given to deliverables produced during the DSDM Atern Lifecycle. A product could be a document, a prototype, an interim solution or the final outcome of a project.
Product Description	A description of the structure of a product, which provides guidance on what the product should contain, its quality criteria and reviewers.

Prototype	A disposable or evolutionary piece of work to demonstrate how an objective has been, or can be achieved. An exploratory version of part of the final solution. The evolution of prototypes through iterative development is fundamental to DSDM Atern.
Quality Criteria	A set of features and/or characteristics against which a product can be tested to ensure its compliance with a stated requirement. Other terms for this are: acceptance criteria; test criteria.
Requirement	A stated business need. A 'function' or 'feature'. Something that the final solution needs to do or exhibit.
Responsibilities	Specific tasks and duties associated with a role
Retrospective	A Facilitated Workshop to look back at the work done over a period, often a Timebox, to assess what went well and what can be learned.
Risk	An event which may have an effect on the project. This can be negative or positive.
Role	A set of responsibilities allocated to an individual or individuals within a DSDM project.
Scope	A description of the aspects of the business or organisation which the project is intended to cover. This could be a list of features and/or a description of areas which may be included in the project (or which may be specifically excluded).
Story Point	A random but comparative measure used to express the amount of effort required to evolve a feature, function or User Story.
TCO	Total Cost of Ownership.
Technique	A part of the DSDM Atern method which is used to help with the execution of a project. There are five techniques in DSDM Atern. These are Timeboxing, MoSCoW, Facilitated Workshops, Modelling and 'Iterative Development' also referred to as Prototyping.

Timebox	A period of time, at the end of which a business objective will be met and a completed product produced. There are different types of Timebox operating at different levels. These are: Project Timebox, Increment Timebox and Development Timebox.
Top-Down Estimating	Estimating using approximate sizings and groupings, where low level detail is, as yet, unknown.
User Story	A requirement or feature expressed from a user perspective.
Velocity	The speed at which the Solution Development Team are working. This may be expressed in terms of numbers of features or story points completed in a Timebox. Metrics related to this across many Timeboxes can help a team to establish a sustainable pace of working.

D. Recommended Reading

DSDM Atern

DSDM Consortium		DSDM The Atern Handbook 2008
		DSDM Atern Pocketbook 2008
		DSDM Atern Estimating Pocketbook 2008

All available from:
The DSDM Consortium
Invicta Business Centre
Monument Way
Orbital Park
Ashford
Kent
TN24 0HB
www.dsdm.org
Tel: +44 (0)1233 501300
Fax: +44 (0)1233 501311

TCC   A variety of downloadable articles on DSDM Atern, DSDM Atern with Prince2 and related areas www.tcc-net.com/agile-methods/articles/

AGILE

Astells D, Miller, G and Novak, M   A Practical Guide to eXtreme Programming, Prentice-Hall, 2002, ISBN 0-13-067482-6

Boehm, B and Turner R   Balancing Agility and Discipline; A Guide for the Perplexed, Addison-Wesley, 2004, ISBN 0321186125

Beck, K   eXtreme Programming Explained, 2000, ISBN 0201616416

Cockburn, Alistair	Agile Software Development; The Cooperative Game, Addison-Wesley, ISBN 0-321-48275-1
Highsmith, Jim	Agile Project Management, 2004, 0-321-21977-5
Kerr, J and Hunter, R	Inside RAD: How to build fully functional computer systems in 90 days or less, McGraw-Hill, 1994.
Martin, J	Rapid Application Development, Maxwell Macmillan International Editions, 1991, ISBN 0-020376775-8
Poppendieck, Mary and Poppendieck, Tom	Lean Software Development; An AgileToolkit, 2003, ISBN 0-321-15078-3
Stapleton, J	DSDM: The Method in Practice, Addison Wesley Longman, 1997, ISBN 0-201-17889-3
Stapleton, J	DSDM Business Focussed Development, 2003, Addison Wesley, ISBN 0-321-11224-5

METHODS, TECHNIQUES and PEOPLE

Ashworth, C and Slater, L	An Introduction to SSADM Version 4, McGraw-Hill, 1992, ISBN 0-07-707725-3
Belbin, RM	Management Teams: Why they Succeed or Fail, Butterworth-Heinemann, 1981
Belbin, RM	Team Roles at Work, Butterworth-Heinemann, 1993, ISBN 0-7506-0925-7
Boehm, BW	Software Engineering Economics, Prentice-Hall, 1981, ISBN 0-13-822122-7
Date, C	An Introduction to Database Systems, Addison-Wesley, 1986, ISBN 0-201-19215-2.
Eason, K	Information Technology and Organisational Change, Taylor & Francis, 198 ISBN 0-85066-388-1
Gilb, T	Principles of Software Engineering Management, Addison-Wesley, 1988, ISBN 0-201-19246-2
Goodland, M and Slater, C	SSADM Version 4 - A Practical Approach, McGraw-Hill, 1995, ISBN 0-07-709073-X
Hix, D and Hartson, HR	Developing User Interfaces: Ensuring Usability through Product and Process, Wiley, 1993, ISBN 0-471-53846-9
ISO 9001	Quality Systems: Model for Quality Assurance in Design/ Development, Production, Installation and Servicing, 1987

ISO 9000-3	Quality Management and Quality Assurance Standards, Part 3: Guidelines of ISO 9001 to the Development, Supply and Maintenance of Software, 1991
Jacobson, I, Christerson, M, Jonsson, P and Overgaard, G	Object Oriented Software Engineering, Addison-Wesley, 1992, ISBN 0-201-54435-0
Jacobson, I, Ericsson, M, Jacobson, A	The Object Advantage - Business Process Re-engineering with Object Technology, Addison-Wesley, 1995, ISBN 0-201-42289-1
Paulk, MC, et al	Capability Maturity Model for Software Version 1.1, Software Engineering Institute, Technical report CMU/SEI-93-TR24, 1993 (Note: CMU is Carnegie Mellon University, Pittsburgh).
Rumbaugh, J, Blaha, M, Premerlani, W, Eddy, F and Lorensen, W	Object-Oriented Modelling and Design, Prentice-Hall, 1991, ISBN 0-13-630054-5
Shlaer, S and Mellor, SJ	Object-Oriented Systems Analysis, Yourdon Press, 1988, ISBN 0-13-629023-X
Symons, C	Software Sizing and Estimating - Mk II Function Point Analysis, Wiley, 1991, ISBN 0-471-92985-9
Yourdon, E	Modern Structured Analysis, Prentice-Hall, 1989.
Yourdon, E and Constantine, L	Structured Design, Yourdon Press, 1976, ISBN 0-917072-11-1

UK GOVERNMENT PUBLICATIONS

CCTA, ISE Library,	Improving the Maintainability of Software.
CCTA, ISE Library,	Estimating with MkII Function Point Analysis.
HMSO	SSADM and GUI Design: A Project Manager's Guide, 1994, ISBN 0-11-330650-4
HMSO	Human Factors Guidelines for the Design of Computer-Based Systems, HUSAT Research Centre, 1988.
OGC (published by TSO)	PRINCE2 Manual 2009 – Managing Successful Projects.

Chapter 1.   Approach and Principles

Answers: 1c; 2c; 3b; 4d; 5b

Chapter 2.   Modelling

Answers: 1a; 2a; 3a; 4d; 5a

Chapter 3.   Roles, Skills and Team Structures

Answers: 1b; 2c; 3d; 4d; 5c

Chapter 4.   Lifecycle and Products

Answers: 1c; 2c; 3a; 4d; 5a

Chapter 5.   Project Management Considerations

Answers: 1c; 2b; 3a; 4b; 5b

Chapter 6.   Facilitated Workshops

Answers: 1a; 2a; 3b; 4a; 5d

Chapter 7.   Requirements Definition and Prioritisation

Answers: 1b; 2a; 3a; 4a; 5c

Chapter 8.   Iterative Development and Prototyping

Answers: 1b; 2d; 3a; 4a; 5b

Chapter 9.   Estimating and Timeboxing

Answers: 1a; 2d; 3d; 4b; 5d